High Heeled Traders

Understand Trading

with Shopping, Fashion, and Shoes!

CHARMEL DELOS SANTOS

HIGH HEELED INC.

This is for my mother,

Mrs. Buena F. Delos Santos,

a teacher.

who valued education so much

she insisted I go to the best schools

we couldn't afford

who taught and showed me and my sisters

the power of high heels

to serve mankind

to love God with song and joy.

Ma, you are the epitome of "fierce"![1]

---

1   *Fierce*—gay/fashion lingo associated with a winning or unstoppable attitude.

Fierce Inspirations and Thanks

To my favorite aunt and godmother, Mama Mena, you gave me so much love and care since childhood. Your humor, intellect, and style inspired me from the beginning. A bold bachelorette at 80 years old, you are still the most elegant goddess of fierceness.

To my aunt, Mommy Coring, the indefatigable glamour girl of fierceness. At 85, you put every fashionista in the malls to shame. (I wonder if getting widowed early got something to do with it?)

To my aunt, Mama Luz, you are money-smart fierceness personified. Thank you for the lessons that you may have unwittingly taught me (including the pastel-colored toothbrush Christmas giveaways for all the kids—fancy, inexpensive, and made every kid brushing happily).

To my aunt, Mama Rosing, you made quiet gentle fierceness cool. I remember the money jar of savings you started on my vacation in your island home, years before you will incur the expense for your son's college graduation. I know you are looking down at us from heaven with pride.

To my aunt, Inang, your yearly visits across the seas and islands is a marvel of sisterly devotion, being the eldest of an orphaned brood in mom's family, you are the "salt of the earth" mother of all fierceness.

To my aunt, LaNay, in New York, we did not spend much time together, but with the little time we had, seeing you in action, I knew your life, as a single mother of four and migrant worker at that, was absolute fierceness.

To Auntie Mer, you helped every one of your eleven brothers and sisters, some even down to their children's children. You are fierceness to the max.

To my sister Ate Gee, I questioned how you can be so dedicated to your craft amidst the chaotic, sometimes murky, world of showbusiness, but your uncompromising pursuit of your passion and creative talent stood the test of time. Your fierceness is truly stellar.

To my sister May, you are the most beautiful of all of us and yet you did not upstage me (when I'm around) even once. Hahaha! Thank you for your fierceness and grace.

To my Dad, your military life could not have prepared you enough for three fierce daughters! Thank you for letting me and my sisters develop into our unique persons to contribute to this world.

Disclaimer

This publication contains the opinions and ideas of the author. It is intended to provide helpful and informative material on the topics discussed. It is sold with the understanding that the author and publisher are not engaged in rendering professional services in the book. If the reader requires personal assistance or advice, a competent professional should be consulted.

The author and publisher explicitly disclaim any responsibility for any liability, loss or risk, by any person which is incurred as a consequence, directly or indirectly, of the use and application of any contents of this book.

Contents

Preface

"You're almost done? Wow, that's so fast!" My colleague Caroline Peig exclaimed when I told her this book is on the final stages of publication. "Last year, you didn't mention anything about writing a book!" I grinned. I remember just being swept along by a wave of energy springing from events and feedback from readers. It's like being magnetized by the word "sale".

I was on my maternity leave in 2010 when I bounced around the idea that trading is like shopping for shoes. Whenever I meet up with girlfriends and monitoring my trades on my phone, almost every time, I get asked about what I'm doing with my trading, or what they think, or heard about it. For example,

- You have to be able to predict.

- Isn't it risky? I don't think I can take losing money.

- How is it different from gambling?

- I have been thinking of investing in shares since the property market is down.

- I have been thinking of investing my retirement account myself.

- How do you manage to do it given the three kids you have to look after?

Most of the time, they want to learn to do it and ask me what and how to study. As we all know, women are different from men, and I thought that the barrier for women to get into trading is how the ideas are communicated to them. If we have references that are easy to understand, then more women would be able to trade. I thought of writing a blog to start my friends on their trading journey while I get the benefit of being able to retain what I learned. I have taken notes throughout my trading journey, feelings, plans, strategies, mistakes, and when I had to lessen my working capital and consequently, the trades I was taking, I thought it was a good time to do it.

I wrote the articles starting from what they should know about trading, gave it a catchy title and opening lines then simply posted them in my Facebook profile and waited for someone to take the bait. It was pretty cool reading the comments:

From Cara T, stylist, Australia

> "Wow i really enjoyed reading this. A fun and easy to understand explanation of trading that also justifies women's shopping habits. Charmel you're a genius!"

From Mariza Sollano Elteibi, IT Account Manager, Australia

> "I'm not going to pretend that I know anything about trading. I was interested before, built a little portfolio. Your writing is great! Coming up with those analogies help women to relate. Hits the nail on the head. Often women baulks at the idea before they even start getting to know trading. You should be commended for opening up the world of trading to women."

From Gay Anne Gaddi, Nurse, USA

> "I'm in! I do have a lot of skills when it comes to shopping shoes...LOL ... I started reading into your writings and trading really looks interesting, and makes it easier to understand from a layman's perspective. I am looking into another means of earning some more mullah, whether i like it or not I'm getting older and   stressed

out with work, the demand physically and emotionally is really taking its toll.   I will continue to follow your writings ...

From Lulette Portuguez, Businesswoman, Macau, People's Republic of China

"Inspired reading your writings....right after praying...so many ideas about ...trading all about trading "business".. making money -sharing ideas."

From Nor Shafarina, Admin staff, Malaysia

"I likeeeeeee... wow u really have good experiences, I admire that! and are u still doing trading? should give some tips!

From Yelitza Martinez, Electrical project engineer, (from Venezuela), based in Sydney

"Trading is like shopping for shoes? Really?! I want to know more!"

From D Robinson, full time mother of 2, USA

"Now I am ready to trade.. this (blog) has a wealth of real information about trading. Your post "What to trade" (a moms guide) was oh so what I needed (as always) thanks again!"

From Fei Dji, accounts payable employee, (from Indonesia), based in Sydney

> "The Right Foundation is actually what I'm looking for to start with and followed by First Things First, the calculation bit. It's a bit confusing but at least I've got an idea what you're trying to say for the very first thing about trading. I think now my part is to "learn" as you said, especially my math, they're lousy ... a lot to learn actually. Your article looked simple & easy to read but well I can say that it has deep meaning if reader cares enough to probe."

It was so encouraging that most of the women are from non-finance background, from different cultures, scattered around the globe. After a while, they would ask questions and how trading can be done along with what's going on in their life. People I don't know also started finding the blog and from there on, I thought this ought to be shared. That there are women out there who are looking for this information and would also find this useful.

I hope this opens up women to the possibilities in trading financial markets, or maybe even help tame that financial crisis!

Acknowledgments

This book is a product of over 30 years of a life with strong women, over 25 years of entrepreneurship and about the same shopping for shoes, 15 years of information technology career, 11 years of investing and trading, 7 years of motherhood, short and sweet 2 years in fashion modelling and beauty pageants, and over a year of writing. My first efforts to get this message out are in a blog, which I, myself wasn't able to find with a search engine, so I thought I'd take the plunge and get this out published as a book.

I received a lot of help and feedback that greatly enriched the contents of this book and made the writing process a pleasurable and fulfilling experience. I would not be able to acknowledge them all by name, so to everyone who contributed in the writing of this book, please accept my unending appreciation.

Firstly, I'd like to thank Dr. Van Tharp, and his wife Kala, Ken Long, Robert Tharp and Cathy Hasty from Van Tharp Institute in the United States, the top organization for trader education in the world, for allowing me to use their trademarked terms and concepts. Van especially, for his life's work, which helped me not only in my trading, but helped me make sense of my journey. Ken, for the many things he taught, but especially for turning on that light bulb in my head on standard deviation, which made me realize I can still grasp something mathematically complicated. You are both great teachers and I am grateful for all you've shared. Robert, the techniques you gave in one workshop helped my confidence tremendously and gave me something to aspire. Kala, I made the first steps of writing for my girlfriends thinking of your words of wisdom. To all the traders I've met in the workshops, for sharing their experiences. I am infinitely grateful to you all.

To my friends in the mother's group, Arum Dhamari, Silvana Kovacevik, Bernadette Jee, Fiona Hue, Estella Roche, for their feedback, support, and trust, that I have something worthwhile to share and encouraged me to start out, my deepest thanks.

To my friend and technical partner, Victor Alexander Debuque of Nuspace Japan, who was the very first person to support my push to get this message out in the world wide web (for free!), my joyful gratitude.

When I had the idea that trading is like shopping for shoes and wrote the first articles with this theme, my wild vision of the chart that looked like a shoe was brought to fine form by my friend, Italian soprano and painter, Marta Ferracin. It has now been registered as a trademark and intellectual property. Thank you, Marta, for lending your artistic talents and having so much confidence in this project. Grazie.

To my dear friend, Lucille Navarra-Ilagan, who is one of the very first persons I talk to about investing and trading and often exchanged stories about business interests, career plans, pregnancy, motherhood, life. She never fails to give me bright ideas to improve or complete whatever I do, she is a project manager beyond compare, she is my foremost promoter and cheerleader. Girl, I could not have braved doing this without you.

To all my friends and readers who gave their time, feedback, thoughts, questions, and support- I could not have written a relevant book for the enjoyment of many if not for all that you've shared. From the past and present, they are my neighbors, colleagues, friends, relatives, classmates, teachers, batchmates, choirmates, girlfriends, and "guinea pigs" in this knowledge sharing. I cited them with their thoughts in this book—a lot of them from the Ship for Southeast Asian Youth Program. I'd also like to thank Arief Mochamad, Somparat Bim Srisantisuk, Warichaya Decharin, Naoko Tanaka, Yukiko Takatsuki, Iyun Witari, Fazlur Rahman Bin Kamsani, Jennifer Mae Ladrido-Luison, Nungky Sari Dewayani, Nisit Palipote, Reena Rose Sibayan, Binky Caral, Cecille dela Pena, Frankie Ong Bata, Sitta Widiasty Murtiningrum, Sukontip Fon Prahanpap, Villamor Bon, Waka

Minamiyama, Murni Budiadi, Juan Agustin Moralde, Masnijuri Andi Palallo, Shalehah Binti Samad, Jonathan Lee. Also to Isaiah Perez, Rev. Fr. Hercks Sambajon, Jewell Capil-Mendoza, Myra Mesina, Joy Verceles Madrid, Lorraine G. Marcos-Werner, Marissa Diaz-Rebulado, Neneng Harmain Jaafar, Beth Casal-Alviar, Pam Albano-See, Raych Gaffney, Roel Lapitan, Dhon Valmores, Criselda Allorina, Ronnie Sosa, Christina Marie, Lanie Vargas Jatulan, Geraldine Sayo, Aileen de la Vega, Carrie Ocampo, Ophelia Mercado, Atty. Minnie Sobreviga-Retanal, Gladys Barbosa, Gilbert Gaddi, Earl Laurente, Ollie Barbosa, Rodenick Barbosa, Reynald Barbosa, Gladys Barbosa, Janet de Asis.

For the beautiful photographs that accompanied my writings, most of them featured in the eBook version of this book –photographers Rev. Fr. Noel Azupardo, and Noel Abejero.

For gamely accommodating my request to model the "little black dress" and killer heels in a photo I needed for illustrating an important point, and the impromptu photo session, Dr. Ging Posadas, you are crazy beautiful. Thank you so much (and I warned you of new stalkers didn't I?)

For providing graphics of the divine shoe images as well as tips about them. Thanks to Rafael Pretto, Eduardo, Taemi and Caroline from the Via Uno Australian stores.

For the book cover concept–big thanks to AJ Mallari, a multifaceted artist, for his insights helping me with the concept and selection of materials. To fashion photographer, John Cody of John Cody Photography in Sydney– I had the most relaxed time in your capable hands-my cover photos look amazing, whatever it is that you did, don't squeal!

For the review comments early on and questions that provided me a framework to work on, my dear friend, Sheila Sanga, thank you for starting me out right, plus through the years, generously sharing yourself, inspiring me to be better in every way, keeping me updated with fashion, and shopping for the perfect outfits for me—tears of joy!

For the very important advice on writing the opening and closing chapters of this book, my dear friend, Dr. Larissa "Dap" Pesimo-Gata, professor of Sociology in the University of Florida and University of the Philippines. Thank you for such significant assistance. I know you've been busy, miss you much.

For specialized content, Architect May Mariano for Urban Planning – thank you for your patience with my questions and giving me the responses I desperately needed.

To Toastmasters Clubs I've attended in the past, Executive Toastmasters Club of Makati (Philippines), and present, Chatswood Communicators (Australia), who helped me to refine my communication and language skills, and above all helping to take away my fear in expressing myself and nurturing my humor, this work is greatly influence by what I've learned from you all. Thank you.

For providing me the most powerful statement that I included in my Conclusion, thank you to 7-year-old Abby Calimaran and to her parents Drs. Arthur and Imelda Calimaran for facilitating everything and Malou Perez-Nievera who introduced us. I read Abby's fun and brilliantly composed article in Malou's food blog "Skip to Malou", so I asked her to write for me. I deeply appreciate all your help.

To Emergen - Australia's community of Emerging Leaders – Janine Ripper and Alicia Curtis, for the finer points of writing in this modern world, the inspiration of the awesome International Women's Day eBook and also Anna Newell-Jones of "AndThenSheSaved" blog for the heartening features of my articles that so motivated me to improve, thank you.

For helping me to think about the marketability of this book–Paul Perez, Dennis Sebastian, Tari Su, Muhammad Hafidz

Zainal Abidin, Antonio Jimeno Jr. and Jennifer Asprec de Peralta, thank you for your inputs propelling me to complete this with the thought that there is an audience that can benefit from this.

For the patient help improving the manuscript and generous rounds of editting, big thanks to my copyeditor Ellen Del Rosario, I insisted on the "hahahas" and smileys, but still you led me to do a professional presentation. To my editor Al Sabado, your diligence is amazing, thank you for catching the many errors in the manuscript and advice that improved the discussions. Finding you both were incidental, I am still astounded with how God worked that out. Special thanks to Maricel Tria (who introduced me to her friend Ellen) and for all the help on content, promotion and resources.

To my younger sister and Editor-at-Large Mary Ann Delos Santos, who is an English Grammar and Literature teacher, to whom I'd often bounce my ideas and whatever I'd write, and my older sister and Editor Extra-Large Gigi Delos Santos-Moraleda, a professional multi-media writer, who have no qualms to give me a tough critique pointing out my mistakes and weak areas – and that photo session I had to harass you both to do for me, I am blessed to have you both, we did it!

To the publishing project team at Createspace, I appreciate all your help and hard work to produce this book with service and speed that exceeded my expectations.

For the very first bulk order for the books–that jolted me to finish the manuscript when I was stuck – my dear friend, Joly Tan, I'm so delighted that you will rock Paris for me! Je suis honore.

To my dear friends Felma Rengel and Dr. Sarah De Luna, Dr. Geraldine Mariano, Mitzi Buhisan David, Priscilla Vergara, Lynnette Antonio, Cristina Allorina Angeles, my very first lady boss Milagros Fe Soliman, godmother Mrs. Lolita Mariano, dear friends in Sydney – Tita Malyn Vasquez, Tita Emma Valenzuela for ministering to me with prayerful conversations and leading me spiritually by your example, "thank you" is not enough.

To the joys of my life, thank you for bringing out the best in me, I cherish our times together and excited for our future. You are my sweetest blessings.

It has been said God uses inadequate instruments for the work to be seen to be His. Glad to be perfectly inadequate for this work. My initial uncertainties to do this quickly turned into enthusiastic resolve with the many people you've sent to help me. Thank you Lord for every one of them and for your grand plan for us all.

Introduction

Just like other traders before me, I would have preferred to be quietly trading and making money without anyone knowing, except the taxman. However, as God had planned life, I realized women are natural traders—and I just have to tell you why… and how!

I was born in a family with strong women role models; my mom is the youngest of seven sisters. Almost all of them were teachers. They got together a lot and liked to huddle in a room where we would hear bursts of laughter and animated storytelling. They like dressing up when they are together; they swap around clothes, makeup, accessories, and shoes—pageantry is in order, even at funerals. Women of leisure they were not, and they taught us business and life skills along the way.

Before hitting my teen years, I worked in the family business of making handicrafts for export to Europe. I was tasked to farm out work to the women in our village and check the quality of their work. The women know nothing of the skills to start with, but a few were taught by my mom, then were asked to teach another, who taught another family member or friend to make more money when we have big orders. Soon we had many workers. I tell you, women can learn anything from each other—and I say anything!

I studied for several years in girls' schools and had my share of modeling stints as well as beauty pageants. And this was what I had observed: women can figure things out. If you can ever learn to put on makeup, then you're golden.

In the mothers' group and playgroup that I presently attend, we frequently ask each other, share knowledge about any tricky situation, and usually get a tried and tested solution. One of these questions asked around is how to get an income while raising children. Little did they know that right at that moment, I was quietly doing my trading—while I was checking my phone every now and then for the stock price. An Indonesian friend of mine, Arum, observed what I've been doing and got interested and my other friends in different parts of the world, asked me to teach them.

At this point in history, we all know that women are different from men, and looking out for references to share, I realized there aren't much trading books offered for women. I became profitable when I traded as woman. I thought I'd share my knowledge about trading using the very same ideas women use in shopping, fashion, and shoes. (So help me God!). Here I will share:

1. What trading is all about. It is not just ideas and numbers; most of it is behavior and actions you may already be doing.

2. The most important ingredient in trading. It is *not* a secret! If you've had success in your life, you already know it and can use it to trade profitably.

3. How your busy lifestyle—children, social life, career—can help you to trade. Have another income and still have a "life."

4. Step-by-step instructions and exact information needed to trade profitably with *low risk*. Avoid the frustration, and save years and money from trial and error with these detailed instructions.

5. Low-risk high-reward trades whether the market goes up, down or sideways.

All these from gems of wisdom (also known as mistakes) that I gathered from nine years of experience as a private investor in real estate, shares, options, foreign exchange, and gold, aided by advanced trading education. I hop around the hotbed of global growth in Asia, Australia, and New Zealand. I started my career as a business analyst in information technology (IT) and that was handy in writing a simple and effective trading process for you to follow.

I started trading because I wanted to be financially free and just do what I love. One of those is to be a mom—for sure, to be a mother is the hardest job in the universe but it is also job with the most rewards. I am not yet financially free, but I only work part-time and enjoy more free time with my three children, get us special treats, and go on holidays to be with my aging parents and family overseas. Not to sound too dramatic, but my trading journey started in Australia, with three pieces of luggage, $2,000 loose change, and 7 of 11 years on one income due to maternity leaves and job loss.

This is for women who have full, busy lives and still have big dreams to live for.

May the Fierce be with you.

Part 1: What Is Trading All About?

I remember when I first started to learn about trading, I devoured books/CDs on "basic terminologies," strategies, researched about companies. I even went on "personal finance" seminars trumpeting "how to get started," paper traded (I thought that was a good practice), opened an account and traded for the first time. $15,000 and 4 months later, I found a hole in my pocket among other things.

Okay, still I stand here at this point with the reflection, that if I hadn't done what I did, I wouldn't be here today. So I am grateful, but I felt if I learned the way or knowledge to start correctly, I could have had better results. I hope YOU don't make the same mistakes. In this part, I would like to offer you the very first things you should know about trading.

Chapter 1: Step Inside

Women Are Natural Traders

In every trading workshop I go to, I count the women in the class and we usually make up 10%. I wondered why—*like it's hard?!* On the other hand, in my playgroup and favorite cafe when they see me checking stock quotes on my phone, many get interested seeing how it can let me earn an income while doing what moms do (bring kids to school, play at the park) and want to learn about trading. And why not? Trading is simply buying and selling. And my belief is that women do this a lot. In our world, this is called *shopping*. I admit the main activity is the buying, but we do get rid of something that has less or no more value. Considering women shop a lot, I thought we would be natural traders! We just don't realize it.

In fact, this could be you:

1) You search high and low, visiting several shops or shopping centers—looking for an item selling below value. Considering the whole scheme of things, you want the item that's selling at a steal. You're a "bargain hunter." In trading, this is called "value trading."

2) You like to buy what is in fashion. Buying "blue"? That is soooo "last year"! You would only go for the new style. You're in with the "trend"; in trading, this is called "trend following."

3) You buy what is not in favor because you know it would be back. In trading, this is called "contrarian," or to a certain extent, band trading (just like rubber band—stretch and go back)

4) You buy when you see a "window of opportunity," or loop-hole. In shopping terms, these opportunities are called "sales." In trading, this is called "arbitrage."

So, you see, there are many concepts that work in trading and shopping that women don't just do but do well. Similarly, the one with the savvy skills gets the goods.

The other thing that should help you understand this whole trading business is that it is like shopping for shoes. Yes, shoes!

1) We should know what we are after. "Oh I really need strappy sandals for a wedding." Just like in trading, start by having an objective. Say you want to consistently achieve 3% of capital per month (36% per year!). If you don't know what you want, where you want to go, YOU WON'T GET IT RIGHT!

2) We buy what is a good fit. Usually, you wouldn't buy a shoe of a smaller size. Like so in trading, if a trade does not feel right for you but you went ahead influenced by someone else, this tends to be a loser. Trade only what fits you, your time frame, trade only the stock/industry you know.

3) We buy a lot! Formal shoes, running shoes, many styles of sandals, boots, according to color, material, etc. You have to have a range of shoe options. The point is, you have to budget for all these kinds of "shoe situations." You shouldn't spend too much on one shoe. So this important lesson in trading is that you have to keep how much you spend at an amount that does not blow out your budget and be able to fund next opportunities.

4) We buy and wear shoes according to the weather conditions. In winter, we usually wear closed shoes so we don't get cold; in summer, sandals are popular to keep cool. Now, in trading, you have to have an idea of what the market is do-ing. Are people optimistic and buying things in the hope of

rising prices (bull market), or are people scared and dumping their assets before the prices go down further (bear market)? Or are people not sure where things are going and there is a tug of war between the people who are optimistic against those who are not (sideways market). You need to determine market condition before deciding on strategy, or choose not to trade when market is too choppy.

5) We buy when we look and feel good. It is easy when deciding for shoes, but it was a surprise for me to know that it also applies to trading. No matter how much the trade looks positive from your analysis, but when you don't feel good about it (or afraid), it won't turn out right and worrying about it can make you cut short a profitable run. This is the worst thing you can do in profit-taking! So before opening a trade, you need to feel good about it. If not, don't trade it.

I can probably go on and on and on, but the other important thing is—as there is always another shoe—in trading, there is always another opportunity.

Sensational Shoes by VIA UNO

First Things First, Why Trade?

What are the first things you should know about trading? Perhaps, we hear news reports about whether the market went up or down, the seesawing of the U.S. dollar, the painful rise of the price of food and gas…and then you "hear" about investing or trading but you don't really know anything about it—it's like a disease—hehehe.

It is in a way related because when you have a disease, especially if it's a bad one, you can't work to earn a living, and that's where investing comes in. Also, in our old age, we "retire" and don't expect to work, so apart from potentially receiving "retirement benefits" or pension from the government, people need to invest and have their money work for them. Investing is like having a (girl) cow for milk and baby cows.

We live in these times where the prospect of retirement is scary; many governments are still bleeding from the global financial crisis, and pensions are in danger of being cut further. My 80-something neighbor says pension payments are not even enough now (and she doesn't even pay rent or loan because she lives in her own house). We help her change light bulbs so she doesn't have to pay $60 for each service call. Every dollar needs to be stretched.

So what do people do? Invest in real estate? Oops, bad example! Well, it used to be a good idea, as people need houses to live in and it appreciates over time. But even during the good times—how many times can one buy a house to invest in? Once a year? Probably not. Anyway, many countries are still in a messy situation due to real estate bought with easy credit, fuelling a boom that has since gone bad. Let's not even go there. Don't get me wrong. I also invest in real estate; however, investments perform well according to the prevailing market. It's like sandals being more popular during summer. Can you imagine wearing boots during summer? Maybe, but you would need a horse to get away with it!

Three Qualities I Want an Investment to Have

A lot of careful thought is needed. You don't just jump into investing. It pays to educate yourself. Read books, go to seminars, and talk to people, analyze, and be critical. After gathering all this information and realizing I don't want to risk too much—I decided to make sure that an investment should have these qualities:

- Protection

- Income

- Growth

I call it "PRING" investing, where the investment performs and lasts in good or bad times.

We can think of this PRING investing in the same light as the "little black dress" (LBD)—usually a simple straight dress that works on its own as an evening wear, you just have to match it with fancy accessories, or wear with a scarf, or with a jacket to achieve a business look. LBDs are versatile and long-lasting; they allow you to have "much" with "little." So remember your LBD when looking for PRINGs.

Little Black Dress

Investing Versus Trading

One of the most successful investors in the world, Warren Buffett, has been consistently ranked by Forbes magazine as one of the wealthiest in the world. "The basic ideas of investing are to look at shares as business, use the market's fluctuations to your advantage, and seek a margin of safety."

It's because of the "market fluctuation"—the prices moving up and down—that people do trading. Trading is simply buying and selling. Buy low and sell high. Or sell high and buy low (as allowed in some markets).

Look at this picture and check the ups and downs.

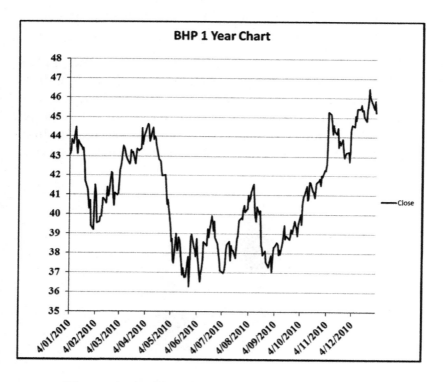

Figure 1: An Example of a Share Price Chart

Buy Low, Sell High

If you were only investing, you would be doing a "buy-and-hold" strategy, which is to hang on to the stock for a long time. Looking at the picture, say in January, you bought the stock at $40, and in November it was at $45. You made $5 per share. Sweet!

In trading, however, you can potentially profit more as the price goes up and down. You need to set up trading rules to capture these profits. Following are the rules that I use in actual trading (I made it very simple here) just to show you trading versus investing.

Simple Trading Rules

1) Entry—You will only open a trade when there is a confirmation to your desired direction.

2) Stop Loss (or "Stop")—You give your trade room to move, and if you are willing to lose or risk (R) $1, we have 1R. If price moves $1 below your entry price, then you get out to "limit" or "stop your loss."

3) Exit—You take profit with a target three times what you are willing to risk; so with $1, you want a profit of at least 3R, or $3.

Sample Trade

1) Beginning January, you expect the price to move up and buy shares at $40.

   a) Your stop is $39.

   b) The price goes up to $43.50.

   c) It starts to go down, so you sell at $43.20.

   d) It earns a profit of $3.20.

2) Say, around February, you buy shares again at $40.

    a) Your stop is at $39.

    b) The price goes up to $44.

    c) It starts to go down, so you sell at $43.50.

    d) It earns a profit of $3.50.

3) Around May, you wait for another chance to buy shares. The price keeps going down, and so you think it is getting cheap. You can't help yourself, so you buy again at $38 without confirmation (violating your entry rule).

    a) Your stop is $37. But because you think it can't go any lower, you don't get out right away.

    b) You get out at $36.

    c) Then you sell with a loss of $2.

4) Around June, you wait for another chance to buy shares, as the price has gone down, making it look cheap. But now you wait for the shares to move up, so you buy again at $37.

    a) Your stop is $36, the lowest price for the year so far, and so you decided to hang on for a while.

    b) The price goes up to $45.

    c) But it started to go down, so you sell at $44.

    d) It gains a profit of $7.

The trading results are as follows:

Profit: $3.20 + $3.50 + $7 = 13.7

Less loss: $2

Total: $11.70

So, we look at an investing profit of $5 versus the trading profit of $11.70. The trading profit is 134% more, and that's just on the upward direction. (You can take profit opportunities with moves going down.) Trading takes a lot of self-control though. If you noticed, not following the "confirmation rule" and the "stop loss" created the "loss." Rules rules!

You can also apply the same mindset of "protection," "income," and "growth" for your money invested in sharemarket by buying shares of big companies. Afterward, trade with a protection strategy and allow the shares to grow and earn income with dividends. Trading can give you more opportunities; if you do it well, you can have extra income…and you won't have to wait until you're 65 to retire!

Trading: Make Money Off People Who Make Money From You!

While I've said trading is a way to multiply your returns through "buying low and selling high" or "selling high and buying low," I mainly think trading is making money with your ideas.

We can form our ideas that will be profitable even just from our everyday lives. Say, I have the idea that more and more people will be able to buy cars. Just look at the booming population in Asia, for example, and India is producing low-cost cars at $2,000, and this means there will be more demand for gasoline to make the cars run. I now have an opportunity to make money from this idea. Big money can buy the oil itself. But as a small investor, I can buy shares of companies that extract the oil or the refiners who process oil into gasoline. I recall the widespread complaints about buying petrol when oil reached $147 in June 2008. I felt protected because I had an oil stock whose price went up along with the price of gasoline. The same thing goes for food. To make plants grow well, we need fertilizer, and there are companies who make it. To fatten livestock, we need corn feeds or other grains to be grown as well. Because population continues to grow and people will need the basics, I can make money from such ideas by buying shares of companies that produce or sell those products.

"There will be more and more ways to communicate" is another idea. Even a fridge can now communicate about not having enough food right? (Now that's a cool fridge!) Nowadays, you can't live your life without a phone and there are companies who make the phone, sell phones, and provide communication services. Another idea is that women are a booming market and increasingly powerful demographic, and so all sorts of products are aimed at women. (See the number of pink cars now?!) By buying shares of the companies aiming to cash in on women's buying power, you can now have a stake in this growing trend. It's like getting a "refund" from buying all those makeup, clothes, shoes, and bling! So trading is a chance to make money off people who make money from you!

To be able to trade, I only need a computer, pen and notebook, and the Internet to connect to an online broker who enter buy and sell orders and holds your funds. To form your ideas, look around you, get education and market knowledge from books, seminars, news, articles, blogs, and newsletters. That's it and all within your control. I am soooooo thankful that this business exists!

Unlike a restaurant business, for example—that is, apart from money—you need people, real cooking skills, food knowledge, suppliers, place of business, advertising to get customers, and so forth, with this type of business, I don't have to have or need to do an inventory of products. I don't have to go anywhere I don't want to be. I was once recruited in a network marketing business, and gosh, I had to travel all the time, even on weekends and at night. I was pregnant then, and I didn't think it was a good idea to be on the road that much. Back when I was active in real estate, there were legal and taxation issues that I really had to pay attention to, as the consequences could be severe. And so I can say that this [trading business] is the least stressful business I have ever done! (Hint: If you are stressed, then you need more trading education.)

As one of my friends said, she wants to learn to trade since [in the trading business] she doesn't have to sell or influence anybody because she's a shy person. Well, you know, I thought I "wasn't artistic enough" to create beautiful products, but I can sell them, so trading is a good fit. There's another person I met, a Jewish guy from South Africa. He is very friendly and has his own store, and he trades because he imports what he sells (he pays for the goods he gets from Germany, Hong Kong, etc. in U.S. dollars) and trades currencies piggybacking on his current business.

Trading is simply making money from your ideas. Or much better, trading is a way to make money off people who make money from you!

The Need to Be Right and Other Myths

As I said earlier, trading is simply buying and selling.

When I first tried to learn to trade, I attended seminars and read books. And the first things they talk about is how to open a trade or "entry" techniques, then comes a parade of oscillators, stochastic variables, Bollinger bands, Fibonacci numbers, and moving averages (i.e., exponential, weighted, etc.). Just hearing these terms already gave me an "indicator overload" and confused the *%r$^ out of me! I guess, for years, I just traded using the simplest indicator (the one that I actually understood, then forgot…), after all, so many myths abound in trading. I write about them here in the hope that it won't stop you to learn to trade or altogether get messed up!

Here are my favorites.

Myth 1: The Need to be Right

The reason why entry techniques or the use of indicators is so popular is that traders have a need to understand, a need to explain, a need to be right. In Dr. Van Tharp's book, *Trade Your Way to Financial Freedom*, (p.46) I picked up the idea that, being "right" has very little to do with making money. Traders think they can control the outcome of their trading by knowing everything there is to know before entering a trade. The truth is, after entry, the market will do whatever it is going to do—hahaha!

Discovering this idea is so liberating. I don't have to "sweat the small stuff" trying to understand and explain. So in my trading and as part of my preparation, I read the news to know what is going on in the market or what has happened in the share price. But I always give myself room to move; after all, I can be wrong. (Don't tell my children.)

Myth 2: It's a Risky Business

Risk is found in every worthwhile activity. A life-saving surgery has risks. Driving has risks. Even a pleasurable activity such as shopping has risks. (What overspending?!) The key is to understand and prepare for the risks that mostly relate to the lack of self-control.

My favorite analogy with risks is comparing trading and driving. Let's see how one gets into trouble with both:

1) Not focusing at the task at hand

2) Not following the rules

3) Overconfidence

In trading, it is worth mentioning that you make rules that are right for you. If you don't have a set of rules to follow, then stop trading; work out the system and paper trade. You've been warned! I made this mistake too, and my company was a "non-profit organization" for years.

Myth 3: Losses Are Bad

Do you ever get a telemarketer from a big company (I'm tempted to mention a pesky one here) calling to offer you a "special deal" and yet you still don't want it? Calling you just cost that company money because of the time, staff, and tools it used to contact you and try to make a sale. That's a loss. And yet they are still in business (woohoo!). Somehow, the telemarketers generate a sale from other leads. Same is true in trading. You don't have to always win in order to be profitable. You have to make losses a part of trading. The key to trading is to keep losses small and make a winning trade's profits grow as big as possible. So spend a lot of time learning and mastering profit-taking "exits," rather than "entry" strategies that get so hyped up.

Say you have $10, and for every trade, you spend $1. After 10 trades, you have 7 losses of $1 and 3 gains—1 of $3, 1 of $5, and 1 of $6. You lose 7 times, amounting to $7; however, your gain from 3 trades is $14, which gives you a total profit of $4, or 40% of equity. Compare that with a term deposit here in Australia, the highest in the world (in 2011) at 6.5% annual rate. What is not to like?

Chapter 2: Trading Success Is in You!

The Right Foundation

Now, you must have seen those celebrities in magazines with full makeup looking perfect. Sometimes, a "natural look" reveals they also have skin imperfections and are mere mortals, albeit with better foundation. I remember my excursion to get a good one; I swanned into the counter of one cosmetic company and met 30 different kinds—at least! Liquid, pressed powder, moisturizing, deaging, oil control, covers uneven skin tone, long-wearing, natural skin perfecting, mineral enriched, matte or luminous finish, full or sheer coverage, etc. The beauty consultant probably saw how overwhelmed I was, so she told me to just try one. With a few trials, we found the one I am happy with, that is, liquid formula to even skin tone for normal skin type with luminous finish in honey. Now that's genie in a bottle!

It reminded me that to get it right in trading, one has to get the right foundation. You need to bring together *what you want* and *what you have* to set a good basis for your trading business.

Know What You HAVE

Consider what you HAVE that affects your trading:

1) Psychology

2) Risk tolerance

3) Resources

   a) Time

b) Money

c) Skills

4) Market beliefs

Psychology

Personal beliefs—imagine the result if you go on trading or any pursuit and believe that YOU CAN WIN! You would be so full of energy and enthusiasm that you do any work the best way you can! You would get roadblocks but they don't stop you because you know you are still in your path to success. You only need to learn to get around them! However, if you think you are "not good enough" (e.g., "I don't have the right education," "I am not good at math"), then this will stop you even before you get started, and you have to change that. You have to hang on to ideas that will help you achieve your goals. Believe that there are always opportunities in trading. Believe in abundance. This is deep, spiritual stuff right here!

Risk Tolerance

I mention "trading" to friends and some say "it's risky." But come to think of it: everything has risk. You could be enjoying an ice cream cone with the risk of drips on your nice clean shirt. You would still eat ice cream right? You just need to be careful.

Anyway, I thought that when I started, you have to take high-risk trades to get high rewards. I have good news though: low-risk trades make successful traders. Now, the following are the things you can do to be careful:

1) Measure risk. When considering a trade, measure if the risk is worth taking. I follow the professional traders' rule of thumb that you only enter a trade that has the potential to give you three times what you risked. So, let's say if you

are risking $100, then the reward potential should be $300. You need to be careful not to just enter a trade. If the reward potential is not there, then it is not worth the risk. Step away.

2) Know what the risk of the investment is so you can decide if it's acceptable to you. For example:

   a) Small companies (either small-caps or "penny-stocks" shares) usually get listed in the stock market to get funding for growth. They are cheap so you can get in with only a small investment (say at 50 cents, your $500 can get you 1,000 shares), which can rise in value compared with your investment (e.g., it reaches $1 in a year so you get 100% gain). However, there can be no earnings and/ or lots of debt. Also, due to its small number of shares, it can be hard to get in and out of, so there's less opportunity to trade. The worst that can happen is you lose your entire investment. Potential reward is *growth*.

   b) Big companies (big caps or blue chips) can provide income by paying regular dividends. They have cash/assets that exceed debt (at worst, their assets can pay their debts, and whatever is left is distributed to shareholders). They grow by buying smaller companies or start other ventures and have large number of shares, which makes them liquid, that is, easy for traders to go in and out of trades, ensuring you have plenty of opportunities. Potential reward is growth, opportunity, and income.

I consider the bigger companies *low-risk*, and so they are the ones I trade. In addition to growth, income, and opportunity, I can apply strategies for protection, further lowering my risk, and increasing returns/income. (I am talking about "options" on shares—fun stuff for later!) But big companies can fail too for various reasons that usually relate to management (e.g., Enron, Nortel, One.Tel). So you still need to be careful and do your monitoring regularly. From learning about the markets, you can also formulate other "low-risk ideas."

Resources

Think about the available time, money, and skills that you can use to do your trading business.

1) Time

First, you need to spend time to *learn* to trade. This includes acquiring the market knowledge, creating a system to guide your decision making on how to place your trade (online or broker), and ensuring you trade effectively with a psychological and business plan discussed later.

Second, you need to know the time frame you would be comfortable to trade. Starting out, I recommend that you adopt a "short-term" time frame for trades (few days to a month or so). Day trading requires a lot of skill and knowledge that one can only learn over time. On the other hand, if you go "long-term trading" right away, you'd tend to be slack and lose focus to do the "trading tasks" and you'd possibly lose interest and money that way.

Finally, for actual trading, the time requirement is minimal. I do short-term trading—and I would normally prepare to enter a trade at a "quiet time"—this would vary from person to person. But for me, this falls on weekends or early in the morning. I spend between 10 to 30 minutes reading the news and doing my analysis. When a trade is already in place and I only need to monitor it, I check the broker's website; it takes a minute to three minutes each time, during which I could be at the shop, at home, at the workplace, or at the park with the kids. I adjust my activity according to the market; if it's too volatile, then I monitor more closely. If I am not comfortable trading (alongside other activities), then I don't trade.

2) Money

This is a big topic. So for now, let's just focus on what you need to think of when you start to trade.

a) **Allocate.** You need to keep the money for trading/investing separate from any savings, commitment, or any living expenses. To trade profitably, avoid any pressure on your capital or "unrealized profit." Some people recommend investing 10% of your income. But I leave it to your judgment to assess your overall life situation. Listen up! Starting out, honestly, I recommend allocating an amount that you can afford to lose. Scary, yes, but since you are new to trading, you might lack the self-control for most part of it and lose your capital. I know this because I did it and got totally wiped out. (Nope, I didn't cry over that. Okay, maybe just a little bit....)

b) **How much?** Here in Australia, I look around banks advertising *term deposit* that offers 6% per year for a minimum deposit of $5,000 for 12 months. So, if you are chasing profits or returns on your money for more than 6%, you should have more than $5,000. Starting out, I recommend going for this amount, although I will discuss other considerations later in the section "Money Matters."

Let's say minimum trading capital is $7,000 that you can afford to lose. For other countries, check my website www.highheeledtraders.com for recommendations.

3) Skills

You will find that skills in computer, research, and math are helpful in trading. If you do not have these skills, learn them. I didn't think I'd be proud to admit one day that I was made to take remedial math, after my passing college admissions test showed that I had too many mistakes in the math section. I had to sit an extra class at lunchtime to learn arithmetic and percentages. In trading, these basic math skills are needed, and some statistics will help you advance. I used to have a blank look at the mention of "standard deviation," but a very good teacher (Ken Long from a Van Tharp Institute workshop I attended) showed us what it is used for and that made it interesting. So, just think that as you get more knowledgeable, you will appreciate this seemingly complicated math.

You can practice much of your basic math skills when you come across signs like "30%–50% off" during shopping.

Market Beliefs

Okay, so markets do go up and down—sometimes slow, sometimes too fast. It's crazy! I won't pretend to know all of the reasons behind these. But I can tell you this: there are ways to profit in an up, down, or even sideways market. Dr. Van Tharp is fond of saying, "You don't trade the markets; you trade your beliefs about the market." So improve your market knowledge, which can form beliefs, which you can, in turn, use in your trading. It helps to observe a "real" market (no, not the supermarket); just look at the chaos! Different people are there together, with different purpose bringing different things. Just like in the financial markets, there are the individual "mom-and-pop" investors, day traders, long-term investors, and fund managers. The governments also get involved. Some may buy and hold, while others are hedgers who want to protect the value of their assets. Likewise, there are speculators who hold positions according to their expectations of rising or falling prices.

Markets also have a rhythm; there is a lot of activity at the start, closing, or at the end of the week. One of my beliefs (from what I've observed on one stock I trade) is that its price tends to go down by Friday afternoon. Funny, it is like one of my favorite things to do at the markets—going to the flowers section near closing time because they tend to sell at big discount, sometimes even for free.

Know What You WANT

Objectives

When I started out in trading business, I just thought I "want to make money." I can tell you that did not help at all, as that did not give me a clear direction. To help define your start, think it over:

1) What is the money for (a holiday trip, a brand new car, or simply a monthly income)?

2) How much?

3) When do you need it?

   Regarding your capital:

4) Do you want to make as much money as you can?

5) Do you want to ensure you only lose a certain percentage of your accumulated capital (i.e., capital and profits)?

6) Do you want to preserve a certain percentage of your original capital?

As regards your business:

7) Do you want to manage your own money and few others (e.g., with family/friends) or just your own?

8) Do you want to be a professional money manager?

9) Do you want to be a mechanical trader or have fully automated trading systems?

10) Do you just want to protect the value of your business and other assets?

Dr. Van Tharp's book, *Trade Your Way to Financial Freedom*, p. 47, has an excellent chapter about writing your objectives to *start* your trading. After all, if you don't know where you want to go, how can you get there?

Time

Do you want to trade actively or prefer a slower pace? Some markets lend to "fast" trading, like the foreign exchange market (or forex). If you don't care for fast-paced trading, then stock market might be better-suited for you, but this also varies according to sector, capitalization, etc.

Market

Do you want to trade a particular market that suits your interests (e.g., from your travel or other business)? Back when I was starting, I didn't know that I could trade country-specific funds. I thought at that time that if you have any such interest, you could only trade forex. Now there are even country exchange-traded funds (ETFs). If you migrated to another country as I did, you must be aware of the value of U.S. dollar against your currency, and this kind of trading could be a good fit for you. If you prefer to trade something familiar, you can start by trading "household name" companies such as your bank, the retail companies where you shop, the bills you pay (e.g., electricity, phone), the makers of the goods you use a software, PC, or even daily needs such as milk or food items.

To Wrap It Up

If you are still reading this, I'm happy for you! Let me just wrap it up here. Most women I know don't want anything "risky." So here's my hard-earned wisdom on getting "the right foundation" for low-risk trades.

1) There is a lot of money to be made in trading. But like anything in life, you have to earn that by developing your skills and taking responsibility.

2) Give yourself time to learn. At the start, you will make mistakes, but keep learning and improving.

3) Aim to preserve 80% of your capital. Also, around halfway of hitting this mark (or after five trades, whichever is safer for you), it's a good time to check how you're doing (performance) and making adjustments to how you trade.

4) Only do low-risk trades. If you lose sleep over it, it's not low-risk enough for you.

5) Aim for a monthly income target. This is a measure of how good your skills are and how consistent you've become.

6) First do mechanical trading, even doing calculations by hand, it reinforces your learning.

7) Devote at least two hours per week to learn. You can surely do more; but contrary to what others might think, trading is not just theory and numbers. A lot of it is behavior. So, go ahead—observe and learn from life. Picture someone who got angry and did something they'd regret because they lost control. You will understand later how life relates to trading. (Hopefully).

8) Trade short-term time frame. This does not put much pressure on yourself, and the trade can still move in your direction.

9) Trade what offers you the most protection. Choose the one that's interesting and easy for you to understand. And for most people, this is the sharemarket.

10) Start with a minimum of $7,000. If you don't have this amount, then build it up while you keep learning.

Whew, give yourself a treat and chew on this one for a while.

It's Not Me, It's YOU!

My friend Dewi (not her real name), who volunteered to be a "guinea pig" of my "trading-for-women" learning program, told me that when she read about my background, she thought business is in my blood, like it's easy for me. I heaved a heavy sigh on that one. To me, it's like blood, sweat, tears, and perhaps, some other facial fluids!

Tell you what, my background was no big advantage. It was even a disadvantage because I was too opportunity-oriented rather than "risk-aware" especially in the beginning. I started to learn trading skills from scratch, and so can YOU!

I tossed around for a while if I should tell you—as in here and now—about the most important factor in your trading success. After all, nine years after I started this business, it really didn't sink in until a few days ago *just how important* it is to make it the cornerstone of every trade I do! There are tons of materials out there, but a lot of them push ideas on "cutting-edge entry strategy," "secrets to win in the market," and more. I am sure a lot would be persuaded by the arguments, and tell you what, most of them *can* work!

The financial markets are part of a dynamic, complex environment where anything can be accommodated and be profitable (at one time or another). But what is the most important factor in achieving a consistent trading income? That is the question!

I am reminded of McDonalds. Do you know what makes the money for McDonalds? "Yes! Sure, heck, why do you ask this question?" you would say. McDonalds is known for hamburgers.

But wait, is the hamburger the money-maker for McDonalds? Aha! Think, think, think! Ray Kroc, founder of McDonald's, aggressively built the business in 1955 with a solid, industrial mode system. It's the one that can even have high-schoolers run the business and make your order to exact standards (where the hamburger sold in Brunei has the same look and taste as one sold in Berlin). However, with all the money being made by the hamburgers produced from such a system, they also have facilities for research, development, and training. Add to that the expensive and unrelenting advertising campaigns. It was said, "It's just breakeven." It has been revealed in business schools that what made money in their business model was the real estate owned by the corporation where every store stands and franchisees pay rent on. That became a consistent income that got McDonald's on a firm foothold into the Dow 30 (formally known as the Dow Jones Industrial Average [DJIA], or simply, the Dow)—the top 30 American companies, by value, that indicate the strength of the American economy. And so it pays to know what consistently makes the income.

Now, let's go back to the trading business. I talked about trading as buying low and selling high. In an earlier chapter, "First Things First: Why Trade," I outlined a set of rules to do trading, which is an example of a simple system. It is basically a shortcut to decision making in the areas of seizing an opportunity and when to get out and make the most money from it. However, just like the McDonald's example, it will help you run the business, but it does not make the money. Especially when you are just new in the trading business, you need to create, *follow*, review, and improve your system. In all these activities, the one that is always present is YOU. YOU are the most important factor in your trading success!

In my case, I have developed a fairly effective, yet simple, system. For six months, the result was a profit 40% of my capital (target was 60% per year); the system delivered like a dream, as I consistently followed it. Then I went to a seminar and excitedly tweaked it with what I learned (without testing), and the result was a nightmare. Other stories are about lack of self-control. My system, for example, told me to risk $200 only, but as I stared at the prices, I didn't follow the stop loss, so it ballooned to a $600 loss. On that same trade, get this, I have a set of procedures, but I didn't follow it because I was just too excited to jump in, as the price has moved in my favor, and I haven't done the complete risk assessment called for in the procedure. It turned out the move was short-lived and reversed, but I could have captured a good move had I chosen a strategy for a longer time frame (a step in my risk assessment). I remember that day was near the close of the month and I wanted to "prove" that I was making a consistent monthly income. So there, my system is fine. I was the one who didn't follow it.

I said earlier that it is so important that I really have to make it the cornerstone of my trading, in every trade I do. I like to call it *self-mastery*, doing when something needs to be done and NOT doing when it is not supposed to be done (self-control). Some call this "trading psychology." I have heard about people saying that in bringing out one's best, "think like the rent is due tonight" or that "there would be no food on the table"—like you're pressured to perform. That doesn't work in trading.

You don't go out and chase profits. You patiently wait for the opportunity, seize it when it comes, and drop the trade when it is unfavorable to limit your loss. But when the market moves favorably, sit back and allow it to reach your target or move it further till the market reverses and takes you out. All this combination of waiting and acting is necessary in trading. That's why I say, self-mastery (i.e., doing and not doing at the right time) is important in consistently making the income from trading. Sounds like a smart shoe shopping to me, don't you agree? You don't just go and buy any shoe, you try it on, walk it; if it looks good but hurts your feet, think about it more and move on to try another one. You can try five shoes and it's time well spent. Then, there's the price factor: Is it worth it? You need take a look and think it over; if it really feels good overall, then you buy it. I told you there's a lot of women's shoe shopping wisdom useful in trading!

So, how do we achieve self-mastery? I think it starts with being personally responsible. Know that mistakes were made and go about analyzing what went wrong and what should have been done or better. Being guided with that, do the right action that the situation requires. You also need to be in good health, body and mind. The thing that I like doing that does good to both is to take long walks. I prefer to go early in the morning. It gives me the exercise, relieves stress, clears my mind, and helps me to reflect, pray, think things through, and be positive.

Physical well-being is a big topic that I am sure has lots of coverage in the media. So help yourself to those resources in the meantime. My main strategy in this area, apart from walking, is to eat fresh! Mental well-being is a delicate topic that I can only refer you to the best resource I know—Dr. Van Tharp has this covered in the Peak Performance Home Study Course as well as in workshops that start with Peak Performance 101.

My short and sweet advice to you in mental well-being is this: *strive to be happy.*

From Damsel in Distress to Goddess

I touched on objectives a couple of times before. Like when we buy shoes, we should know what we want (e.g., "Oh, I really want new shoes for the wedding"). It helps so that you don't get distracted (like when another non-formal shoe "is on sale"—be strong girl, be strong…) and not spend your resources on "other" things that don't fulfill your objective. Say your objective can be to consistently achieve 3% of capital per month; that's a total of 36% per year! Since we are taking baby steps to trading, know that you won't get to this right away. One of the first objectives I recommend is to *learn*. You will be making mistakes. But that's natural and that's how you learn. Then there should be a sense of "graduation," as you gain knowledge and skills. Just so you know, professional traders (who manage other people's money) are viewed to be doing a good job when they generate upwards of 20% regularly for their clients. I personally see three levels to this:

1) Profitability—your ability to add to your capital

2) Consistency—your ability to add to your capital regularly

3) Alchemy—your ability to profit excessive returns with low risk at the right conditions. (I mean, you know, this is goddess-like powers!)

Profitability

I remember reading the book, *Trade Your Way to Financial Freedom*, by Dr. Van Tharp and thinking that the concepts in there, not discussed in other books elsewhere, are very powerful. I was convinced to trade using ONLY his concepts. I put together a system from the "ingredients" presented in the book. I remember I had about six months trading, and after that, lo and behold, I made 18% of my capital—with a lot of human errors too (meaning I did not follow the concept or how I should be using the system). It's probably not a marvel, but 18% beats bank interest rate anywhere!

Consistency

Let's go back to the subject of retirement. If, at 25, you put your money—say $10,000—at a bank that pays 6% interest, it will be $102,857 after 40 years. That doesn't seem much, does it? Now, let's take my example of being profitable by 18% with the same $10,000 after 40 years; that will amount to a staggering $7,503,783! Now that sounds like we have a major amount of money now, haven't we? So, imagine that if you consistently make 18% from your trading and investments, then that will really make a difference in your life.

Check out the Investment Returns Table I posted on the website http://highheeledtraders.com Book page.

Alchemy

In the olden times, alchemy was practiced to turn cheap metals into gold. I have cited it here to represent making excessive returns from low risk. To do that, one has to have the knowledge and experience to know when the situation could be ripe for such opportunities. Legendary trader and investor George Soros made $1 billion, making a massive bet against the British pound sterling when he correctly anticipated that the Bank of England would have to devalue their currency. (I was just researching about him again, and I found that he actually wrote the book, *The Alchemy of Finance: Reading the Mind of the Market.* There we are!) In my case, I have found that these opportunities do exist when back-testing. Now, I just need more knowledge and experience to actually see it before it happens.

Let's Do It!

So now, let's focus on our number 1 objective: To learn to have consistent skills in investing and trading. I'm excited! Are you? If it helps, I'm going to confess that early on I struggled in learning to trade. I mean, no one wrote an easy-to-read book for me to follow! I had to lose some brain cells trying to understand finance books; when you also get to read a lot of them, you'll find that they're conflicting or they confuse the heck out of you!

Anyway, I just know I have to do it, so I just kept going. I remember my friend, a very nice woman who is newly retired with her husband who was a builder. At the depths of the financial crisis two years ago, she told me that she got a report from her financial planner that their "retirement account" is down by $80,000. She was shaking. Now, I don't know about you, but $80,000 is a big amount to me! Come to think of it, it's kind of funny that we let our financial lives be run by these "professionals." We assume that since we don't know much about finance, they do. I say assume nothing!

So it's worth spending time on learning to trade and invest, if only to know how to choose financial professionals to whom you would be entrusting your money. Don't be among people like Steven Spielberg, Zsa Zsa Gabor, Larry King, Kevin Bacon, and many private and public organizations who lost money when he entrusted millions of funds to Bernard Madoff, a former head of NASDAQ electronic exchange. Madoff ran a scheme for decades, scamming people billions of dollars in life savings. There was a suspicion that his returns are not mathematically possible, but it was not proven before he admitted to the fraud, when his clients began redeeming money during the global financial crisis.

If the "professionals" are not doing a good job, you know what to do. Find another one or do it yourself! Let's get ready to learn.

Chapter 3: Learn to Last

What I'm going to tell you is probably something not discussed in most trading books. I know there are books about "secrets," "edges," and other marketing buzzwords. But guess what, they missed this topic!

Trading, is a fluid or sometimes erratic business. Yep, it can get crazy. So you want to learn what will help you to be profitable (not lose all of your money, first of all) and eventually, with the right skills, to go for the stars! So the very first lesson I ever-ever-evereverrrrrrrr—want to share with you is to learn to last.

Here are a few things that help me keep going:

1) Financial concepts

2) Psychological well-being

3) Physical activities

Learn to Last Financially

I started to attend seminars on financial freedom after starting to work in information technology with long hours and getting slapped with high taxes. It has been very valuable to get financial education through books, seminars, and people who talked about their experience. Not all of them might be useful, but it helps to analyze the information. Doing so will improve your knowledge and sophistication.

I came across three concepts that greatly helped me in my trading and investing, as I started out with very limited funds.

1) Velocity of money

2) Infinity

3) Position sizing™

Velocity of Money

The "velocity of money" is an economic term that the St. Louis Fed (a part of the U.S. Federal Reserve System or central bank of the United States) defines as "the rate of turnover in the money supply" or the number of times money is used to purchase final goods and services (included in GDP). For example, a hairdresser and a dentist have $100 between them. The dentist goes to the hairdresser every month for a haircut worth $20 every time. The hairdresser has teeth cleaning done every six months and pays $100 each time. For one year, together they made $440 from their services, with $100 to start with.

When we started in Sydney and lived on a single income with limited funds to use, I hung on to this idea every time I looked around for a potential investment. I thought I should aim to use my one dollar several times to buy my investments. So when investing, use a combination of products or strategies, aim to get your money back quickly, and use it to similarly buy and create another investment. Do it again and again and again. You can do magic with this idea!

Infinity

When looking at an investment, we calculate how much we can get back; we meet the return on investment (ROI) or yield. This is under the presumption that we still have the money invested and it is "returning" money back to us. What about if we don't have money invested anymore (we've taken it out already), but we still hold the investment and we still get money coming to us? Wow! That's a return of *infinity*. This is an old, old, old concept in mathematics that means "no limits."

Try this: take the calculator and get the ROI. For monthly rental income, put in $150 multiplied by 12 months and then divide it by zero. What did you get? Mine says, "Can't divide by 0." That's because the calculator has no imagination. But we humans are equipped with great minds to make money from nothing.

Position Sizing™

As you can see, I've had to put the letters "TM" after the word "sizing." That is to denote that this term is a registered trademark owned by the Van Tharp Institute. In my opinion, this subject should be one of the *very first* concepts that traders should study because it would help traders to survive the learning process. I lost all my capital in three months when I first started to trade. The account balance just started to dwindle when I lost on my trades and eventually got wiped out.

To make it easier, think that it's like buying shoes. (Really?!) We buy a lot! We buy formal shoes, running shoes, boots, and countless styles of sandals according to color, material, etc. We have to have a range of shoe options for our lifestyle.

The point is you have got to budget for all kinds of "shoe situations." You shouldn't spend too much on one pair of shoes. So the important lesson on trading is that you have to keep how much you risk at an amount that does not blow out your budget and still be able to fund next buying opportunities.

Position Sizing™ is a way to determine "how much" to risk in any one position. To clarify, this is not the amount you spend on a trade. This is the amount you're willing to lose for that trade. You decide on this prior to trading anything; tell yourself how much you are willing to lose per trade as a percentage of your capital. And when you are just learning, the "how much" should be small so that you preserve your capital while still be able to profit from an opportunity. Say for example, you have $5,000; you want to preserve 80% of your capital, or $4,000, you then have $1,000. Of this $1,000, you want to budget for a string of losses (say 10 consecutive losses), which will give you $100 to spend in a position. (Fees are excluded here for simplicity.)

$5,000—capital

$4,000—amount to be preserved, at 80% of capital

$1,000—amount to be risked at trading opportunities

10—the number of successive losses you are willing to tolerate

$100—the amount you will risk in a position

$100 or the 2% of $5,000—your position size

Is this a small enough risk for you? A hundred dollars is already 2% of your capital. If not, you should probably build up your capital, gain more knowledge, and test your system and skills until you are comfortable to spend this amount.

Position sizing, a concept used to preserve and grow capital, is discussed extensively by Dr. Van Tharp in his book, *The Definitive Guide to Position Sizing*™. He also has a free trading game that can be downloaded from www.vantharp.com.

I will show how to use these three financial concepts to get you started on trading profitably in the section "Show Me The Honey." Let's first discuss other concepts that you need to understand to apply them.

Learn to Last Psychologically

"Cut your losses short, let your profits run" must be the most repeated phrase in trading. And if you're new to this, trust me, don't argue with it. The biggest mistake that you could make is to make a small loss balloon to a big loss. The other one is to make a small loss balloon to a big loss. I know, because I did it and got wiped out.

Okay, first let me tell you—if it isn't obvious in what I've written so far—that in the business of trading, *losses are okay*. Nobody told me that in the first years of my trading. One of the psychological preparations that you should learn to last in trading is to accept that losses are part of the trading business. That is, small losses. I repeat: *small losses*. I touched on this in "The Need to Be Right and Other Myths."

Come to think of it, losses are part of doing any kind of business. Think about this: a business, to be successful, needs customers. Attracting customers is also expensive; for every 30 contacted, only 6 may sign up and the business lose money on the 24 that didn't. That's the reason why companies have "loyalty programs." They want to make the most money from the customers that stay with them. The same thing goes in trading. You have to tolerate 24 small losses of say $1 each, or $24, but make the most of the winning trades. Six trades could comprise two trades of $3, one trade of $6, two trades of $7, and one trade of $10 for a total of $36. Spending $1 for each trade, or $30, you get $6 in the end, which gives you a return of 20% (excluding fees). The key to trading is making the most profit out of winning trades. So "cut your losses short and let your profits run."

TRANSACTIONS

2 trades with profit of $3 = $6

1 trade with profit of $6 = $6

2 trades with profit of $7 = $14

1 trades with profit of $3 = $10

24 trades with loss of $1 = $24

Total profits = $36

Total loss = $24

SUMMARY

$36—value of winning trades

$30—amount spent for 30 trades at $1 each

$6—profit

0.2%—return on capital

When You Lose BIG

To analyze the mistake of making a small loss a big loss is not a simple one. Psychologically, it could involve a number of reasons: not accepting a small loss because of "ego" (i.e., you don't want to admit when you're wrong); you're "hoping" that the move will return to your favor; you feel important when you get sympathy over the loss; or all of the above. (Oh, noooo!) One major loss I had was a result of being "distracted" because I was on maternity leave while taking care of three kids all under five, my world was confined to home, and I was missing family and friends (you know, adult interaction). I got too involved with trying to catch up with loved ones overseas in social networking. Wayyyyyy toooo much!

After the major loss, you're allowed to feel bad if you really feel that way. I've learned in Dr. Tharp's Peak 101 workshop that it is healthy to feel your feelings rather than suppress them or go in "denial." In your case, as in mine, you might find a deeper reason as I found out later. This is the time to be honest about issues that keep your focus away from doing the right thing. We all make mistakes. The important thing is you recognize your mistakes that led to runaway losses. You take personal responsibility, seek to learn from the mistakes, and improve through them. Then you have to free yourself.

My friend Kriengsak Senaworaprasit shares about a beautiful ceremony in Northern Thailand called the Yi Peng festival. Traditional belief has it that when huge hot air balloons are set adrift, so do the troubles of the persons who launched them. Say goodbye to bad feelings.

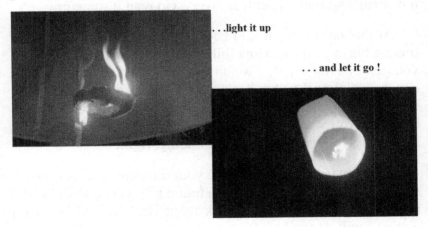

Thai Lanterns by Kriengsak Senaworaprasit

Do this regularly: talk to yourself, learn, release, and take care of your needs. As mothers, it is our job to take care and nurture the children. But often, we forget to take care of ourselves, as in, we are the last in everything. As I found out, we take better care of people around us when we ourselves are happy and whole. If you need to go get some pampering or a little excursion (to the mall?) to keep yourself from snapping, then do it. (Okay, so you know this already? Good!)

After Getting Wiped Out

Hopefully, you don't get to the point of being wiped out, but if you do, I've been there and I have handy hints ready. Try these:

1) Eat

2) Pray

3) Love

Sounds familiar? *Eat, Pray, Love* is a book and movie about a woman's journey of self-discovery. Go read it sometime.

At this point, you would be really thinking and deciding if trading fits in your life. Hopefully, as part of your self-discovery, you get to recognize that we all have our need to achieve security, financial well-being, heck, even just managing money matters for our everyday lives. Because that need is there, it's got to be filled. You want to take charge of your financial well-being that's why you were looking into trading, right?

Being a "trader" might not be your ultimate goal, but does it still fit in your life plan? I'd been trading for years when I had a miscarriage, which made me think about life. I decided from then on that I will do the best I can as a mom, and to provide for the needs of my kids, I will be a trader. I even started calling myself "trader mom." So you can see me bring my children to school, to the park, and to playgroups, shopping, running errands—at the same time monitoring my trades through my smartphone. (I prepare before that though.)

A trader I met is a passionate mountaineer who wanted to climb Mt. Everest. He started to trade to raise funds for the climb. He now manages money for his family and friends.

It must be a natural consequence that once you get to have good results in something like trading, you learn more and get good at it. It is entirely possible to *add to what you already are*: a fascinating creature of many and superlative talents and achievements. Multidimensional! Diamonds have nothing on you, girl! (Let's talk ourselves into it!)

Now, going back to trading again after losing all of your money, I want to share with you the three things that helped me: progression, motivation, and prayer.

Progression

I lost so much money early on when I first started trading. If there was one consolation, it really cemented the fact that people can make serious money from trading the markets—the people who are more skilled than you. Although I heard that people return to trading to get back what they lost (like with a stroke of magic their money will return to them). My main reason for going back to trading is the realization that "I made a lot of mistakes that I learned from, and if I don't go back to trading, I am throwing those lessons away." Though it was painful in the beginning to have lost all that money, I'm glad I did it since I knew I learned a ton, got "out of my comfort zone," and made progress on something where I really want to succeed. Isn't that good? Treat the loss as "pruning" from which new life blossoms.

Motivation

Since you're still reading this, I presume you really want to learn to trade. Yesssss!!! Here are some of the ways to build up your courage.

1) Heroes. These are the people whom you can look up to and learn from because they have gotten successful in the field.

   a) Billionaires Warren Buffett and George Soros are known to be über-rich, influential investors and traders.

   b) Have you heard that American star basketball player LeBron James has been consulting with Warren Buffett? Talk about being multidimensional.

   c) John Keys, prime minister of New Zealand, built his fortune from being a forex trader.

2) Check what's missing in the above list. Women. Very few women trade, and it's a shame. You could be the new heroine for women traders! You go, girlfriend!

3) There are the usual activities that give us the natural feeling of being positive. The list is long, but here are my favorites:

   a) Music. There are just "anthems" that make you feel powerful—"We are the Champions," "I Believe I Can Fly," and "Don't Stop Believing" or any upbeat music that will get your energy going.

   b) Walking. I love this exercise; it helps me to clear my mind.

   c) Art appreciation. I don't know why but the sight of a beautiful painting, sculpture, dance, or dress just gives me so much inspiration and heightens feelings of my own capabilities.

   d) Family and friends. These are positive and honest people who inspire, support, appreciate, and encourage you to give your best.

   e) Every day, I start with prayer, goals, affirmation, and gratefulness. This routine is part of my preparation work in my trading process, discussed at a later section, "Step by Step by Step"

Prayer

One of my current favorite reads is written by J. Alexander (also known as Miss J, the 6-foot, 6-inch-tall, black queen in America's Next Top Model). In his book, *Follow the Model*, (p.96) he wrote:

> The idea that God helps those who help themselves really does work. And the operative word there is work. You have to be willing to work hard, and if you do, other people aren't going to be the only ones who notice. The universe does too. I don't know how to put it much plainer. It has always worked that way in my life and my friends' lives as well. Complaining and bitching about your situation will get you nowhere in life. No one wants to hear it, least of all a Higher power who has got more important things to do than listen to somebody whine without taking any action.

I hope you get to last long and learn enough to reap your rewards of trading.

As my Muslim friends say, *Inshallah* (God willing).

Learn to Last Physically

With the exception of disc jockeys, voiceover announcers, and phone-sex operators, most jobs out there are physical.

I know you'd think there is nothing physical about trading (I didn't think so too), so let me enlighten you. In studying to trade, we already have physical demands, squeezing it in busy days at work, taking care of family, traveling/driving, or even socializing. In actual trading, we have to make timely and competent decisions that bring about a very common physical challenge to traders, that is, stress. A lot of traders get stressed with losses as well as the constant pressure to absorb news or developments in the market, particularly for very active traders. Lack of energy is another problem that affects trading. In making decisions or in monitoring the market, your tiredness can also distract you as well as your self-control. We do have to have a sound body to have a sound mind.

Here are my top tips to last physically in trading:

1) Exercise

2) Eat fresh

3) Rest

Exercise

This topic needs no introduction, so I'll just tell you my favorite way to exercise: long walks. Besides the physical workout, your mind is set free when you walk. I use this time as well to think of what I learned. Sometimes, I am able to connect two ideas to help me in my trade and it helps me plan what I need to do to build up my capital. Sometimes, it makes me realize the risks more. The entire thinking and physical processes meet up when I walk—it's multitasking heaven.

Okay, so now, in keeping with what I've written here, I am going to squeeze in discussing shoes. Well, because I have to warn you about wearing the "wrong" ones! There was a time I was walking, doing all those wonderful thinking I told you about, when—whooooops!—I tripped, fell, and sprained my ankle. That must have been caused by the pair of shoes I wore that day—one of those "new" ones in the market that elevate or make you rock back and forth. (Don't make me name names!) When you are out in the street or outdoors, the path is likely to be irregular or uneven. Use shoes that are low, comfortable, and let you balance easily even when your mind is wandering.

Eat Fresh

This one is another familiar topic, and there are lots of resources already out there. So, I'm just going to tell you my top tip: eat fresh food.

For years I've been planting herbs that I conveniently pluck and enjoy in my salads, stew, or soups. Last summer was the very first time we planted tomatoes in our balcony, and it was wonderful! The children just loved watching them grow, bear fruit in bunches, and change color from green to orange and red. The very first time we ate those red ripe tomatoes, I could feel and taste their healthy goodness—so fresh, no chemicals. I felt like I could live up to 150 years old! My mother's family (she got sisters who are over 80 years old) are all still strong and spritely; they love eating vegetables and fruits that they mostly like to grow around the house. My parents, who had retired in dad's island hometown, enjoy fresh fish every day and are spared many illnesses from high-cholesterol food. You actually get the most vitamins and minerals eating fresh food. Most vitamins "dissolve" with water, fat, and when heated, and so the cooking and processing of food you eat rob you of their healthy goodness. So have a diet consisting of a lot of fresh fruits and vegetables. It helps to juice or put them in a blender and drink it when pressed for time or for the children to enjoy. We also cut fruits and veggies in small pieces and eat them while studying or playing (my daughter calls this "munch and crunch").

Rest

During summer here in Sydney, the sun is still up until 8:00 p.m. So oftentimes, we go to the beach around 6:00 p.m. and get stunned to find that the car park is still full! And who can blame them? The wind from the sea is exhilarating, and there is something just so invigorating sitting down to marvel at the power of the waves and sheer majesty of the clear, blue sky. It was beautiful, beautiful, beautiful.

It only takes two hours to travel and relax at the seaside, yet I feel that I had another store of strength for the next 126 hours of my week's waking life. Yes, a little time spent with complete peace and rest gives your body and mind more focus and energy that you will need in trading and everything else.

Of course, not everybody can go down the seaside in minutes. Here's a few other ways:

- Breathe. Slowly. Deeply. One…Two…Three…. Combine this with relaxing your muscles and good posture. If you are sitting, pull your shoulders back and straighten up your spine.

- Listen to soothing music. Just go for your slow favorites. Mine is instrumental piano and guitar.

- Meditate. Close your eyes and let your thoughts float.

- Get a massage. Or you can do this yourself throughout the day by applying slight pressure with your fingertips on your forehead and shoulders. Use scented oil like jojoba or infused virgin coconut oil if you like.

- Lie in a warm bath with herbs. Rosemary, oregano, and flowers are aromatic treats that make you feel gorgeous.

- Look at pictures that make you smile. Photos of happy faces and enthralling landscapes are sure winners!

- Hug someone you love, soak in that pure joy and innocence.

Notice that you can do any of these as quick or as long as you want. If you find yourself in a stressful situation, for example, if the U.S. market breadth is negative (this means more companies fell than gained), then it is likely to influence your session's trading. Before starting, relax yourself, do some breathing exercises, and just follow your system. Get out at the designated stop, or if the move is in your favor, be patient, follow the market, don't let your excitement cut your profit. Your body will be more responsive to your thinking when it is rested and relaxed.

Make It Happen

All these activities for physical well-being I listed above need time. How do you make it happen? If you are one of those people (like me) without much help available, then you just have to do all that you can and keep moving forward. Stay motivated, be efficient, and get others to do things for you when possible (I've taught my then six- and four-year-old kids to do their own beds when they wake up in the morning). Also study or trade in the best time for your "body clock." I discuss how to fit trading in your lifestyle in a later section, "Get Trading, Get a Life."

Till then, chill, baby, chill…

Chapter 4: Making Money in the Markets

Let me say it again, trading is a way to multiply your returns through "buying low and selling high" or "selling high and buying low." Also, trading is a way to make money from your ideas.

Therefore, as mere ideas, opportunities can come and go on the "markets." Now, let's step back a bit. A "market" is the same thing in everyday life; it's where buyers and sellers meet. There's a general market (with "everything") or a specialized market (e.g., fish market, flower market, produce market of fruits and vegetables). These days, we can even find online markets such as eBay and Trading Post.

I think back my days in the Ship for Southeast Asian Youth Program when we visited seven countries in two months. I'd like to check out the markets in every country we visited. The markets are a bright contrast, and it can be a disadvantage to people living in "developed" societies not to have the daily scenes of a market. When we need something, we go to the "supermarket" where there is only one seller, so they just post how much they want for something and that's it. Not fun at all. Being exposed to a market culture, you can readily see the market in action. There is movement and even chaos. Prices go *up* when there are a lot of people buying, *down* when too many sellers are eager to sell, or sideways when there is uncertainty. Prices can also be *quiet* when there are a few participants (e.g., low volume of buyers and sellers).

It is often a very fluid situation at the short term on any financial market. And so I like to think about the financial markets as oceans that resemble the real world oceans—they are distinct (e.g., Indian, Atlantic, Pacific) and yet they are one (interconnected).

Let's Cruise: Markets to Trade

Here are some markets (or investments) and the opportunities they present.

1) Stock market/equities

2) Bonds

3) Foreign exchange

4) Commodities

5) Derivatives

6) Funds

7) Real estate

Stock Market and Equities

The *sharemarket* is a venue where company's shares are traded. An investor who wants to place his/her money while expecting capital gains and/or regular income (dividends) can buy shares. Each share represents ownership of a company's assets less its debt (net assets). A company issues the share for owners to cash in on their investment or make it grow. After the first issue (initial public offering), they are traded in the stock market so that people can get in or out of the investment.

You will also hear about the "exchange" that is responsible for matching the buyer and the seller who should both transact in the same exchange. This is because a company can be listed (available for buying/selling) in more than one exchange. For example, Sony, a Japanese company and maker of electronic goods with worldwide presence, is listed in the New York Stock Exchange and Tokyo Stock Exchange. So an investor buying

Sony stock in Japan will transact with an investor selling stock in Japan, and the Tokyo Stock Exchange will match them.

Bond Market

Bonds are debt investments. Governments and companies issue bonds to finance their operations. So if you invest in bonds, you are lending your money to them. In exchange, you get regular interest payments and you get your money back at a certain time called "maturity." Bond market is usually made up of institutional investors (like banks), governments, or a sprinkling of wealthy individuals. These days, if you want to invest in bonds, you may do so through an investment bank or join a pool of investors through a "mutual fund," also known as ETF, as discussed below.

Currency Market/Foreign Exchange (Forex)

Wayyyyyy back in history, when trading of goods and investment went beyond territories, a way to convert "currencies" was devised. After all, the buyer and seller have to agree on the value of item being traded; say silk, which could be 30 dollars, is about 50 dinar. A currency is used by a country (or a group of countries) to enable the exchange of goods and services. The forex market is the biggest in the world, averaging $3.98 trillion *daily*, which makes it very liquid (or easy to get in and out of) and attractive to traders. The forex market presents opportunities: (1) gain from the increase in value of one currency, (2) get more return from interest rate payable on your funds when converted to the currency of another country, or (3) both! It has been said that *money will go where it is treated best*. Australia's official cash rate is hovering at 4.75%, the highest among the most developed (and least risky) countries, while Japan's interest rate is 0% to 0.1%. Where will your money earn more? You do the math!

Commodities

Physical, raw, or primary products are bought and sold in standard contracts available in commodities market. Examples of these include agricultural products (e.g., corn, soybeans, cotton, wheat, sugar), energy products (e.g., crude oil, natural gas, heating oil), and precious or industrial metals (e.g., gold, silver, platinum, iron, copper). The economic situation also affects the movement in prices, as poor economy results to lower demand and dampens the prices. In times of crisis, some commodities like gold and oil tend to attract investment, as they are considered "safe haven" or critical asset. Commodities trading involve physical delivery of the product, although, thanks to the fertile imagination of finance professionals, other financial products based on these investments, like derivatives are now available to be traded (see below).

Derivatives

These are financial contracts whose value is "derived" from an underlying asset (e.g., share, currency, commodity). The common types are swaps, futures, and options. Traders use derivatives for leverage (e.g., profit from a move in value using a small amount of cash). They speculate or take profit if the value of the asset moves as expected. They hedge or protect from risk, especially when they hold the asset and participate in a trading opportunity when not possible physically. For example, oil—if you don't own a warehouse, you can't take delivery of barrels of oil. I trade options on oil shares; apart from the benefits mentioned above, I like the idea that I can earn an income while protecting my stockholdings, effectively lowering my risk, and increasing my returns. It requires a bit of study, but it's helpful to lower your risk and is worth the effort. Totally! Options are discussed in a later section "Keep Your Options Open."

Funds

Investors can put their money together into "funds" with other investors to invest in assets. A fund manager employed by an investment firm manages the money. You might have heard of "mutual funds," "hedge funds," "pension funds," or "exchange-traded funds" (ETFs). Among those mentioned above, ETFs are the only funds traded in the stock exchange. ETFs provide profit opportunities for an investor where he may not be able to do so alone. For example, buying gold ETF instead of physical gold when you don't have a huge sum of money or storage, or country-specific ETF that can let you profit from strong growth in companies doing business in countries like India, Brazil, Indonesia, or South Korea. ETFs are sold in units, are traded like shares, and are allowed limit orders. You can short sell (first to open transaction and close by buying it back) and carry out options trades.

Real Estate Market

Of course, who can forget real estate? It is just not popular now, but people borrow and still put money in it. After all, we all need a place to live or conduct business. There are many kinds of real estate investment: residential, commercial, and rural property, among others. There are also "group investments" such as property syndicates, real estate investment trust (REIT), and so forth. Rental income from tenants and capital gain from increase in land value are the main reasons to invest in real estate. Do you hear that? Not "the tiles were a beautiful sky blue" or ornate fireplace or you'd have a chance to pay less tax. Alarrrrm bells! If you are being enticed into investing in property harping about the tax benefits, run away! Real estate is just not too profitable at the moment because of the global financial crisis, but banks used to advertise their willingness to lend 100% to buy a house. Party's over!

Check out Appendix section for a comparison of investment in real estate and trading.

A Super Ocean

This finally brings me to say, I believe that all these markets are interconnected, as they affect each other's performance or movement. I mentioned the idea that "money will go where it is treated best." If you have any doubts about this, just think of retirement. By then, you won't or you can't work, but the income has to come from somewhere. So to provide for the future early on, money is placed where one can get the best returns. Say at 25 years old, you put your money in a term deposit account paying 6% over 40 years, with compounding (that is, it keeps adding the earnings to the original amount). An initial $10,000 investment roughly becomes $102,857—the amount you are supposed to live on for the rest of your life. Say another 20 years, it's not enough is it? That's why you need to keep adding on your retirement fund and make sure you get the best returns.

"And where are the best returns?" you might ask.

The information age has made it so easy to know what happens in other parts of the world. Just before I went to sleep one night, I checked the markets, and Europe's stock market was down due to debt issues with Portugal. There was fear that the government cannot pay back their debt (the bonds lent by the investors). Then I woke up with gold moving up at $4.50, considered a "safe haven" from weak currency or too much "wild swings" (volatility) of either euro or the U.S. dollar. The U.S. market, which opens following the European market, fell 100 points at the start of the session, when seemingly, it recovered because there was some upbeat news about U.S. companies, but more companies fell than rose and the session still ended lower. Big money could move to invest in growing economies with less debt worries—Indonesia, Thailand, Vietnam, or the robustly growing India, Brazil, and China. That's why U.S. companies that get a lot of revenues from these markets also report high earnings, which excite the stock market.

Okay, before anyone runs out to invest, I am just describing what happened in the markets within 24 hours; the up and down moves are not predictable. One time, there was even a very poor jobs report in the United States but the stock market moved up 100 points and kept inching up for two months because it is believed to justify the U.S. government's spending to stimulate the economy—a case of "bad news is good news."

In May 2010, the U.S. market plunged 10,000 points in a matter of minutes and recovered in a matter of minutes. People offered different explanations, like someone with a fat finger entered a wrong trading price, and following that, technical sell signals were triggered by computer programs. Eventually, months later (and even after government investigation), no one figured it out.

All right, so these markets move a lot and affect each other. This leads me to share what I've learned—that the financial markets is like a vast, complex, dynamic super ocean. I spent countless hours trying to know everything I can, with no spectacular result. It turns out you don't have to. It does what it does. I think women can easily accept this truth, just like when a man you shared a few good dates with gets cold, "he's not that into you."

As a trader, you don't need to know everything about the super ocean that is the financial markets; you just need to know how to *ride the waves*.

Riding the Waves by AJ Mallari

Buy 1, Take 1: Market Types and Strategies

With low prices giving you "more bang for your buck," we all look forward to buying the things we want and "saving money" on sales. As a seasoned shopper, you probably know that this is "temporary" and should seize the opportunity. And as a bonus to us girls, we can definitely use shopping skills in the investment world! Yes, investments go on sale too or ride a hot trend. It's not a secret, but few people would be brave (or knowledgeable) buying on these "sales season" at the financial markets, when stock prices go down and company valuations are "cheap." Then, situations change and some markets could get attractive again due to growth prospects; markets "rally" or creep up gradually in cautious optimism. Yet again, there are times when some are positive about the market, others could find less reason to risk. In this case, there is a seesawing or side-ways movement in the market.

So before doing any investing, you need to "know the different conditions" you could find and know that each condition needs different strategies. Please, please, take that as a "buy 1, take 1" advice! It breaks my heart every time I read about this or that "secret" or "strategy" that is promoted at full blast without equal emphasis on when they are suitable. No way! It's like going out in stilettos everywhere! Cannot! Think, when going out to the gym or a walk, sport shoes are essential protection and are needed to get the best benefits of the physical exercise. In the same way, *for every market condition, there are appropriate winning solutions.*

Animals Roam

Bulls, bears, and chickens. You would come across these "animals" in the financial markets, although I have to warn you,

you wouldn't read "chicken" in financial materials elsewhere. I just thought I'd add it here because we all know not everything goes up or down, black or white, left or right. Do you hear what I'm saying? No? Okay, just read on.

Bears

They say bears tear "down" their enemy or prey with their paws; hence, *bears* are used to describe investors who have a negative view of the market, pushing prices down by selling. When a lot of people have this negative view, we have a "bear market," meaning the market is on a downtrend.

Bulls

The bull, on the other hand, would fight with its horns going upward; hence, it's used to describe investors who have a positive view of the market, pushing prices up by buying. "Bull market" then means the market is going on an uptrend.

Chickens

Well, in common language, we say someone is a "chicken" or "chickened out" when tentative, unsure, or quick to change his/her mind. In financial markets, when there is a lot of uncertainty, this causes prices to move or swing more (become volatile); therefore, people are quick to take profits, in case the market reverses. There is a tug-of-war between the people who are positive and negative about the market; hence, the market would move sideways.

These things are worth repeating here, and I hope you realize the importance of investing with these market conditions in mind. What are you going to invest on or trade that will still be profitable in up, down, or sideways market? Usually, this is the more "liquid" assets or markets. "Liquid" means how easy you can get in or out of an investment. Also, in addition to where you invest is the strategy you can apply to profit from the market moves and be protected.

Going for the Catch!

All right, so what strategies could work given the market condition? Here are some examples.

Bull Market

This is the easiest market to trade, usually by buying up-trending assets.

- Buy and hold. With this strategy, you buy an investment that you can keep for a long time. It's not a bad strategy if you bought one that's very cheap, say, when the stock is newly issued or at the bottom of the bear market if you were fortunate and skillful enough to have done so. The *Motley Fool*'s Foolish Four approach is an example of this strategy, which recommends buying Dow 30 shares and holding them for a time. Just remember, you still need to set a "stop loss" or a limit to tell you when you will get out of the investment; some investors' newsletter such as *Investment University* recommends to set a stop at 25% off the highest price.

- Buying call options. A call option is just a contract that allows you to buy at a price you want at a future date. With options, you only pay a small amount for the contract that lets you participate in the move of the investment.

This will be discussed in detail in "Keep Your Options Open."

Bear Market

You need to be careful because few assets can be traded in this downtrending market.

- Short selling. With this strategy, you sell first at a high price and then buy later at a lower price. The broker will facilitate the transaction by borrowing the asset from another owner. During the height of the financial crisis, short selling on some companies' shares was not allowed by the U.S. and Australian governments in an effort to keep the markets afloat.

- Buying put options. A "put" option is a contract that allows you to sell at a price you want in the future. "Keep Your Options Open" also discusses this in detail.

Sideways

The movement in this market does not last long. One day, the market could go up 200 points, and then the next day, it goes down 150 points, depending on the news or economic reports. Sharp moves can happen in different time frames, and a profit can quickly turn to a loss. As a private investor, remember that *you can step away* when the conditions are too choppy.

- Straddle. This is an options strategy that combines "buying put" (for the down move) and "call" (for the up move) at the same price. For example, a stock is priced at $15 and you think the price could have a massive move up or down from this price. Say you bought a put option and a call option, then the price moved to $25; your call option will be very profitable (say a profit of $10), you lose on your put option (loss of $6), and you then make $4.

Options are discussed in detail in the section "Keep Your Options Open."

To emphasize this lesson on knowing the conditions along with the best strategy, let me give you another example. Remember Dewi, my friend who wants to learn about trading? I suggested that she do some research and gather information. She later sent me back her notes on an article in one of the finance websites she found. The author recommended to "Buy shares at regular intervals (monthly or every two months). If the share prices are down and you buy the same shares, you would bring down the average price of the shares." This strategy is called "dollar cost averaging," which works fine in a bull market, but if every month you buy shares in a bear market, then it will become "dollar cost hemorrhaging." Why? Because you keep buying shares that do not go up, and your original investment is at a loss. Then what's the point? You'd just keep on bleeding and eventually give up on it.

So remember, you need to know the different conditions that could happen in the market and only use a strategy that will perform in those conditions. And yes, it's like sandals to keep cool for hot summers, then thick, cozy boots to protect you from cold winters—bet I didn't have to tell you that!

Chapter 5: Dressed to Trade!

This is the moment of truth. Now, let me tell you what you are getting into in the trading business. It requires a lot of knowledge and activities intricately woven together. But, as we girls can dress up to be "well-put together," we can do this! It just requires careful and advance planning—something worthy of a hot date!

Starting Preparations

Know Thy Self

Hot date or not, you owe it to yourself to know who you are and to present yourself accordingly. In the same way, trading requires self-mastery. You trade based upon your preferences and your limitations, and you should respect that by making sure you exercise self-control and not overdo things (discussed earlier in "It's not me, it's YOU!"). Self-discovery can take you to a few journeys where you will learn more about yourself as you trade; so be patient, don't expect too much anytime soon.

Set Rules and Follow Them

In dressing up, you would have "style rules." Is your dressing style conservative, sexy, or casual? In the same way, this requires decision-making that's easy for you when you go shopping (like easily eliminating low-cut blouses, if you are conservative). In trading, you need these rules put together in a system as a short-cut to get into trading opportunities. This includes the following:

- Know what type of market is prevailing currently (i.e., bull, bear, chicken) and adopt a strategy that will fit.

- Know the risk and the cost per trade (i.e., position sizing)

- Know what will pass as a profitable opportunity and when to get in (i.e., entry criteria).

- Set a limit to losses when things don't work out (i.e., stop criteria)

- Know when to get out with your profits (i.e., exit criteria)

These are discussed in the earlier chapters, "Buy 1, Take 1," "Why Trade?", and "Learn to Last Financially." Review them as needed.

Practice

You wouldn't debut a fake tan or a never-tried-before hair color to a big event. First, it may not really flatter you or go with your overall look. In the same way, be careful not to plunge into trading with an untested system and self-mastery skills. Give yourself time to craft how you will operate your business, practice using your system, and then evaluate your performance while practicing. It is also important to plan for fail scenarios (just like keeping lipstick with you to touch up), so that you are well prepared when things move against you. Girl, I can assure you, this preparation is essential, and it's better to lose "play money" than the real thing. Just think, you could have been shopping or going on vacation!

Dress Up!

1. Get Clean

I hear this part of a song from my mom who came from an the Ilocos region in the Philippines: "*Nag*-lipstick *kangaag*-lipstick *di ka naman nag*-brush your teeth." Roughly translated, it says, "What's the point of putting on lipstick if you haven't brushed your teeth?" Eeeeewwwwww.

In trading, you have to start every trade with a clean slate.

Ken Long (http://kansasreflections.wordpress.com) from Tortoise Capital calls this being on a "zero state." You are not excited or frustrated so that you have a clear mind and you see things as they are. Only then are you able to make sound decisions in trading. Therefore, it is essential that you renew yourself for trading every day.

2. Hair

As in our everyday life, deciding about the length of your hair requires careful consideration. For example, I like to grow my hair long, but it is thick and got a bit of wave. So I need to invest time to take care and groom it; but with three kids, I don't have much time!

Hair length is like a time frame where one's suitability to temperament and lifestyle is a major consideration. The same thing goes in trading.

- Day trading. Your transaction is quick, in and out on the same day; this will require constant watch when the trade is in progress.

- Short term (swing trading). The transaction can take a few days or months. You get more flexibility in what you can do while checking the trade few times each day.

- Long term. The transaction takes a few months or years as long as your stop is not breached. This will only require monitoring at the end of the day.

In terms of performance, not one is better than the other because success depends on the trader's abilities. For baby traders, I recommend the short-term time frame or swing trading. Regular and constant monitoring of the market gives you more knowledge and chances to develop your skills.

3. Foundation and Makeup

Present yourself well with good skin. Thanks to a good foundation, your "genie in a bottle" making your skin look perfect! Getting this right is a combination of what you WANT (e.g., liquid, matte finish) and HAVE (e.g., oily skin, mature skin).

I have devoted the section "The Right Foundation" to discuss what you WANT and HAVE that would form the foundation of your trading. Here's a rundown:

What you WANT

- What are your objectives? How much money do you want to make?

- How will you operate the business? What's the time frame? Will you be taking clients?

- What market do you want to trade if you have specific interests?

What you HAVE

- Psychology

- Risk tolerance

- Resources (time, money, skills)

- Market beliefs

And what about makeup? *There is no point in putting make-up on if it doesn't make you look good*, right? Usually, the best use of makeup is one that emphasizes your good features. As in makeup and as in trading, play to your strengths, what gives you an advantage—and this includes what suits your time frame, interest, temperament, and whatever powers you have!

Foundation and makeup – get it right!

4. Underwear

Let's explore the basic purpose of this garment:

- Protect the body and prevent unwanted exposure.

- Achieve a certain mood (ooohhh-la-la).

If you do choose to skip this, know the effects and consequences. The accepted norms of society favors having them on in public. (Remember the scandals on a which popstar was that again?). In trading, I would say this is of the same essence as position sizing—never go without!

When you are starting to trade, ensure spending small at 1% to 2% of your capital. This position size will help you to last long enough to trade while still learning the concepts and self-mastery skills.

On the other hand, legendary trader George Soros was said to have recommended that when you have earned the right (for example, 30% above your capital) you can be bold to risk a large amount for a trade to win big. This strategy is to be used sparingly, only at carefully considered big reward opportunities.

Not having or not following a clear position sizing system would result to being overexposed to risk and likely to end trading venture or large losses. I discussed this briefly in "Learn to Last Financially" and in greater depth in a later section "Survive and Thrive: Position Sizing™."

5. Dress

This is the most noticeable part of your look, so make sure you understand how to wear it, that it shows your best. We can once again take a fashion tip from Miss J. Who else? He's the most lovable judge in America's Next Top Model and author of *Follow the Model*, p. 96, where he stressed that "the most important thing is to never, ever, subscribe to one that isn't right for you". For example, skinny jeans are made for thin people and if you are not of similar size, STEP AWAY from the craze. It may be the hot trend, but if it does not make you look good, then find other clothes you can rock!

This is similar to trading a financial instrument, concept, and strategy. You have to understand these fully to effectively trade it. Warren Buffett was said to have missed out when the dotcoms fuelled a bull market in the United States from the late 1990 to

2000. He famously said he does not want to get involved in anything he does not understand. And he was proven right because the dotcoms went from boom to bust in just a few years.

From my experience, since I worked in IT, I tried some practice trades on Microsoft. But I couldn't make sense of what makes it move—knowing about the company's financial health does not seem to be enough.

Then the price of oil was going up and getting painful at the pump, so I tried trading it. I found that I am able to understand oil shares more and what affects the movement. Example, supply and demand, violence erupting in producer countries, as well as relationship with currency trends like the time that U.S. dollar is in a downward trend (oil is priced in U.S. dollar in the global markets).

As with dresses as well as in trading, I must mention that it would be wise to have a strategy in mind like "doing much with little." I used the idea behind the "little black dress" as an example or shopping for clothes that you can coordinate or wear differently in many occasions. To do this, let's trade with protection, income, and growth. I discussed this in "First Things First: Why Trade?"

6. Shoes

This is not nearly as noticeable as the dress, but you will agree with me when I say that it is just as important. After all, this includes "high heels," with instant inches gratifying our desire to achieve a "higher self."

I wouldn't have as much fun writing this if not for shoes. Yes, indeed, many trading lessons I share here have been compared to shoes.

Here's a rundown (from earlier section "Women are Natural Traders"):

- Objective. We should know what we are after.

- Buy something that is not only a good fit but also the one that blends with your time frame and interests.

- We buy a lot! So, take care that we don't blow our budget.

- Buy and wear something that is suitable to the conditions.

- Buy what looks and feels good.

- As there is always another shoe, in trading there is always another opportunity.

I probably did not stress this as much before but with trading, you are in the path to achieving your best. We discuss trading success being a fruit of self-mastery when you are purposeful in your thoughts as well as your actions and you channel your energies to something you want to achieve.

7. Mirror

You check your reflection in the mirror every now and then to know if things are what you want it to be. Does the dress drape well and hide the flaws? Has your eye shadow blended well? In trading, the same "check-the-mirror" exercise is required. This is where you would check how well (or bad) you are doing.

- Did you follow your rules for trading? If not, that's a mistake and you should make corrections. If you did follow your rules and still made a loss, that's okay; that's just a part of doing business.

- Are you monitoring your trades so that you know whether it is time to move your stop? Or is the trade moving favorably and you want to make the most money by managing your profit-taking exits?

8. Overclothing and Underclothing (Jacket, Tights, Hosieries)

While these items of clothing are not always worn, they are must-haves for protection in tough weather conditions. In the same way, when the financial markets are going up or down (sideways) too fast, you want to be protected. It pays to implement a strategy that will protect the profits or value of your investment. As an example, I may use the options strategy covered call or buy put option. These strategies are explained in detail in a later section, "Keep Your Options Open."

9. Accessories (Hat, Scarf, Bling, Belt, Bag)

They could all be simple or one makes a statement. Surely, they can be many, BUT they *must* work together. In the same way, a trade gets its reward and is completed with exits. I have read in Dr. Van Tharp's book, *Trade Your Way to Financial Freedom*, and confirmed in my trading that the simple ones are really effective. Yes, you can have many, but make sure they work together. For example:

- Time exit. I give a trade up to two months; if it's not profitable, then I will close it.

- Psychological. I determine when I will not be able to trade due to personal circumstances (e.g., being on holiday).

- Profit target. The critical one, I target three times my initial risk.

- Tighten. When profit target is reached but price is still moving in my favor, I let the move go on. But I tighten my hold on profit by setting a limit to when it reverses and I take profit at that point. Let's say the profit target is $5, moved to $8, but reverses; I get out at $7.20 when the price pulled back by 10% (or 80 cents) to protect my profits.

10. Perfume

Just before stepping out, you would reach for your favorite scent to give you an extra boost to conquer the day. In trading, it is important for you to feel good over a trade. If you are not confident, you can cut short a profitable run because of fear.

I personally think lack of or not following a clear procedure, preparation of self and tools of trade could dent your confidence, so it would help to prepare yourself, and things you need, and then relax. It also helps that I write on my little notebook the things I'm supposed to do in any move I can expect that day.

11. Tools

Looking good has tools: manicure set, hair dryer, straightener, curler, among others. Now, trading has tools too: calculator, computer, Internet access, notebook and pen, filing materials, and storage. A smartphone may not be essential but is definitely helpful when on the move, especially for easy monitoring of your online account. For studying, we need books, CDs, and newspapers for market developments. Online news sites are best because they get updated within the trading day.

Business as Usual

Apart from the trading-specific knowledge and activities I've discussed, here are the usual business components:

1) Understand the nature of the business. Know what you should expect and know the essence of the business (e.g., food + service = restaurant). Trading is about "Riding the waves." Know your obstacles and opportunities.

2) Training and education. Any business or job requires thorough education and skill; trading is the same. Look for trading programs that are comprehensive and are not just focused on a single concept or strategy. I like Van Tharp Institute for advancing trading skills. They have a Basic Trader program as well as Super Trader program, accompanied with all the trading components we've been talking about here.

3) Procedure and operation. What are the steps and tasks required to make your business deliver results (i.e., product or service)? McDonald's is legendary for how it operates in business. We want to do the same thing, which will give us steady results and something that can be done exactly, possibly by future business staff.

4) Documentation and information management. To put it simply, this is record keeping that helps take care of three important things: (1) how you are actually doing things, like filing trading statements to ensure you know the actual price you bought and sold; (2) a record of what you did for self-improvement; and (3) your compliance on tax and securities laws.

5) Organization. While you don't need a staff for your trading business at the start, it pays to know the other people that may be affected or involved when you are trading. I also make sure my trading time frame is suitable for work or for my schedule with my children.

6) Contingency planning. Do you have a backup when things go wrong? Like when you usually trade online and your computer is not working, have phone trading numbers handy, smartphone, or somebody do it online for you. When I was about to give birth to my third child, I cut my active trades but let the long-term ones move along. I asked and showed someone how to monitor the stock price for me.

7) Business structure and taxation. At the start, you'd probably trade with personal funds. If you happen to have a company,

you can trade under a company name too. As you get skilled, you may want to trade and invest on a retirement account or funds in trust for other people who want you to manage their money. Whatever your circumstances, you need a business structure for taxation and protection of assets.

8) Growing the business. This is very important and this is where a small business is differentiated from a big business. With trading, there are no global barriers. I have my online account in Australia, but I am able to monitor and execute some trades even when I went on an overseas trip (to Singapore, the Philippines, or the United States). You can generally open a trading account in any territory subject to their laws. To grow your trading business, you can put in additional capital, get a loan (or use leverage just like buying a real estate investment), or venture into other markets for more opportunities. You can also attract capital from other investors and manage money for them while earning management and/or performance fees. Some of the biggest investments and trading funds are Soros Fund Management, Paulson & Co, and PIMCO—each of which is worth billions of dollars. You can look up to these big money guys and learn from them.

These are prime business considerations in trading—usual for any business.

Trading is major, isn't it?

I mentioned earlier that despite all the studying I needed to do, trading is still the easiest business I ever did. Think of what you don't need to do: manufacturing, quality control, billing and collection, inventory, warehousing and distribution, sales and marketing, legal management, security, physical plant, property management, staffing and human resources, disposal system, government relations, and more! Arrrrgghhhhhh! I can think of more headaches in other businesses compared with trading!

While it seems that trading is such a complicated business, I hope you're convinced that you can do it.

We can get dressed up even though it's complicated putting everything together, and sometimes we do it more than once a day. Get dressed for work, then get dressed to party. Let's get dressed to trade!

Part 2 : Get Trading, Get a Life!

Not too many trading resources will touch on "lifestyle" when discussing trading. From studying to trade, you can learn a lot from how you do your shopping, the fashion, and the shoes! Add to that being a parent, a mother, and a professional that give you skills and insights you can use in trading. Also, the physical aspect of trading is usually overlooked, but I can tell you—you need to manage stress so that you have a clear state of mind to perform well. And the most important lesson of all that turned things around for me is that I need to weave trading around my lifestyle, ensuring that I take care of aspects in my life that give me a sense of purpose, joy, growth and overall wellbeing (and okay, the chores too). Your lifestyle may help give you a clear mindset and overcome stress.

Chapter 6: Trade Up Your Lifestyle

Beginning Trading: A Shopper's Guide

I can't seem to recall when I took my first elegant baby steps in buying shoes on my own. I do remember many shopping expeditions with my mother. So, as I say, "Trading is like shopping, wisdom in shopping is honed for years! So, the first lesson is that learning to trade takes time. Don't expect to learn trading in three months, unless you've totally understood most of the trading concepts I've discussed here. And if you were a savvy shopper, you'd definitely be able to trade profitably sooner than most. But don't rush, okay?

We've been saying that trading is basically buying and selling (and we'll keep repeating this until you say it in your sleep). Sounds simple, but hopefully, you now know that trading is not a business to sneeze at. To make it easier for some people (including me!), think that it's like shopping for shoes. When do you think something is a "good buy," a "bargain," a "steal," or simply a "must have"?

You have your own criteria, right? What influences your buying decision? Is this the hot trend or is it on sale? How much do you spend? When do you need it? What you can wear it with (does it complement what you know you have)? Where are you buying it (market)? These are just some of the trading concepts applicable that any self-respecting shopper understands. Okay, so in the perfect world, you would window shop, try on a few things, and buy following your criteria. But sometimes you don't.

Like when you are in a rush, tired, stressed, too excited, broken up with someone (uh-oh), your mind is clouded. You tend to forget your criteria and just buy whatever, vaguely aware of being able to exchange or get a refund. I'm sure you are familiar with that. Then you go home, pull out the new purchase, and walk it. If it's perfect, you're happy. If it pinches your feet, hurt, or does not work as well as you thought, then you're best to cut your loss and go back to the store to get another pair.

There's also a chance, you'd hang on to it too (yeah, different reasons, too lazy or love the brand, what the heck!). Every time you'd walk past the shoe rack, you know there are probably too many in there (but always have room for one more!) and a number of buys that didn't really work out. (Ouch!)

Lesson learned: You've got to be a better shopper! Long story, but trading, like shopping, is a simple idea. It needs some work but well worth the effort for *best* results.

Trading in Real Life

Previous sections have given you an overview of trading. Here I've arranged them into task groups that I do in real life!

1) Research and education

2) Developing self-mastery

3) Business planning

4) Actual trading

5) Performance monitoring

6) Get back to trading/improvement

Say again? How does trading relate to shopping?

Research and Education: Learning Shopping 101

Girl, before you hit the shops, there are a few points you should know about getting out into the world—as in our case, the markets where people are out to make money. It's learning about what you should know to accomplish your shopping mission. And these are similar to the trading ideas that we've been discussing here so far.

• Market. Where do we get the best deals and the one that we're comfortable with?

• Market type and strategies. Is the market going up? Or is it time to lock in profits and sell?

• What concepts to use. Is there a trend? Are there bargains?

• System (rules) including position sizing. What is a good buy? How much do we spend?

• What moves the markets?

• Other market knowledge.

Self-Mastery: Work-Shop

Here I mean that we should lay the groundwork for trading success! We've talked about self-mastery as the primary success factor for consistent trading. Self-mastery means "doing when something needs to be done and NOT doing when it is not supposed to be done (self-control)." This area in trading is also called "psychology." Before you enter a trading position, remind yourself of the following:

• Risk control. What's your risk tolerance? When do you take the risk, low risk ideas?

- Stress management. Stress will lower your performance, thus you need to relax.

- Attitudes and beliefs. Are you aware of what's driving or stopping you?

- Practice trading. Window shop or trade/shop with no money involved to learn and get comfortable.

- Mental states. Is it a good idea to trade or shop when you are fuming mad? No need to answer that! Don't even think of doing it! It's best to trade or shop when you're in a "zero state" (not excited or frustrated from last trade). This will allow you to see the opportunities as they are and just to make your decisions according to your system and plan.

Business Plan: Mind Your Own Shopping

Yes, the business plan is different for every person, and it would be dependent on each one's situation.

- Objectives. What is it that you want? For trading, this could be the expected monthly income or how much you are willing to lose (e.g., 20%) and preserve (e.g., 80%).

- Money. This includes the funds to commit and the funds to risk.

- Time frame. Is it for long-term, short-term/swing, or day trading?

- Plan B. Expect that things may not go according to plan.

Actual Trading: Ready, Get Set, Shop!

- Look for opportunities.

- Am I following the rules (system).

- Open (buy to open or sell to open).

- Monitor the trade.

- Close (profit-taking exits or stop loss).

- Document and file.

Full actual steps to trade are discussed in Part 4: "Work It!"

Performance Monitoring

Hey, does this trading make me lose weight? How do you feel about your trading?

- Are you able to work and sleep at night?

- Are you too excited?

- Are you meeting your objectives?

- Are you following your rules (system)?

Get Back Up and Improve

Buyer's remorse and recourse

- Mistakes? What mistakes?

- How do you summon up the courage to get back in the market and trade?

We've talked about most of these points, questions, and concepts in previous chapters. Review them. Plus, we'll have more detailed discussions in the next sections, promise!

You may notice that once you've acquired the knowledge on all six task groups and laid out your business plan, you only need to be doing the task groups of self-mastery, actual trading, performance monitoring, and improvement. On a per-trade basis, you will need to be doing self-mastery and the actual trading. Lay a solid foundation for the business and it will be more fulfilling and profitable.

Meantime, keep thinking about your shopping experiences because trading is like shopping, and as I said, they will teach you how to trade. There is a saying, "What you hear, you forget. What you see, you remember. What you do, you understand." Makes sense?

The next chapters discuss how to weave trading into your life.

But before that, let's practice some trading tips in the wild. Go hit the shops! (Enjoy, but shop responsibly!)

Wise up! Shop and Trade

View From the Top

I was looking down at the peeptoe shoe I tried on; it's pretty, but one of my toes was sticking out like a hotdog that's too big for the bread. Can't have that! My shoe size is 8½. I eventually landed on a size 10. Monstrous! I knowwwwwww. But what the heck, it's just a number; I will rather have what fits me perfectly.

That shoe shopping wisdom is definitely a springboard to success in any business. (Who knew?!) Just take a look at Sean "Diddy" Combs, now worth $475 million, the wealthiest hip-hop artist according to *Forbes* article by Zack O'Malley "Why Diddy will be Hip Hop's First Billionaire." Diddy built his wealth chiefly from music, clothing line, and vodka. The article points out that "Diddy makes his lifestyle coexist with every-thing else he's doing," making his wealth building both enjoy-able and lucrative.

Bling It On!

So what do you do with your lifestyle that could coexist with trading? You might find inspirations here:

- Have a thing for bling? Have a look at investing on gold, silver, or platinum, also known as precious metals. More-over, they are a store of value in uncertain times (war, financial crisis) and widely used in modern technology (e.g., phones, computers), thus enjoying high demand. Aside from physical things (jewelry or collectible coins), you can invest on shares or funds that mine and process them.

- Are you the homey type? Then check on investing in banks as well as retailers of food, gardening, consumer goods, home wares. Understand when people (including you) feel confident to spend or borrow for these investments.

- Walk everywhere? Usually, we drive or fly—which burns oil. If the visit to the pump station is getting painful, then invest in shares or funds that produce it to share in the profits from the high demand.

- Love traveling? Learn about countries. There are funds that hold country-specific investments or see how their currencies perform against the U.S. dollar like China, Brazil, or Indonesia exchange-traded funds (ETFs), or take the example of Japanese housewives trading the yen and the U.S. dollar because household budgets are affected by the currency moves.

- Big fan of fashion and shoes? You can definitely check out investing on retailers or companies producing them. If you are of the fiercer sex (and have been reading this for a while), you know what I'm talking about when I explain things we know about shopping, fashion, and shoes to understand trading concepts.

The Perfect Fit

Then there's the question, "How do we achieve consistent success in trading?" With self-mastery! Again, self-mastery is "doing when something needs to be done and NOT doing when something is not supposed to be done (self-control)." You have to take a view from the top and see where and how to fit trading in your lifestyle. This will help you summon self-mastery by maintaining your self-control or keeping yourself motivated in trading even when you're busy with your job or with your children.

I will skip telling you of my misadventures in trying to "find time" or "balancing" life for trading—they didn't work! Instead,

I recommend that you understand and do your best to ensure that the many aspects of your life support trading and the "ultimate goal," which, for most of us, is happiness in life.

Your Life and Your Trading

Make the parts of your life support your trading business.

Spiritual

Totally critical. It helps maintain attitudes that are essential for success in trading or other endeavors. Praying is a step in trading process that I didn't think I need to do for years; however, I found that doing it as part of my trading gives me chance to gather myself together to do my trading effectively, freed from worries or negative thoughts that take away my "clarity." Fundamentally, being spiritual allows us to bring out our best, contribute, and receive in return. As Venerable Master Hsing Yun wrote in *The Essence of Buddhism*, "we should have a joyful, optimistic and positive outlook on life." Be open to receive the abundance of the universe!

Relationships

Good relationships help keep you motivated and the people around you may be able to assist in monitoring your trades or you can even give them some tasks. I know, in my case, having children makes me motivated yet more aware of risks and losses. These realizations help me maintain my self-control in following trading rules.

Work and Career

Use the skills and strengths you already do at work (even in nonfinance roles) that could be helpful in trading. Here are a few examples:

- Medical or health professional. Use emotional control, similar to being detached or dissociated so you make the right decisions. (You can't be emotional with your patients.) Use your discipline in following rules. You can also use your skills in developing procedure, minimizing risks, or increasing efficiency when time or safety is of the essence.

- Administrative or office staff. Use patience and your discipline in following rules and developing procedure or some technical skills at documentation and information management. Filing or organizing can definitely help your business.

- Sales/marketing people or entrepreneurs. You know what's hot in the market so you can use that in selecting the investment/shares you want to trade.

- Artists or sports people. You can certainly use your drive to study and commit to practice for the best possible outcome. Having imagination on how you can win will greatly help too.

- IT, engineering, and trades people. Your strength in analysis, breaking things down, and problem solving is handy for analyzing opportunities and developing solutions and procedures. Remember sticking to rules; discipline counts massively as well.

- Teachers, mothers, and other fields in human relationships. Certainly, using patience, your ability to act when required (flexibility and self-control), and your being conscious of contingencies (you bring extra nappies and clothes in case something happens!), you don't want to risk a lot. But you do want to develop procedures for high efficiency.

If you notice, I didn't mention any content or knowledge you'd have to have, that is easily acquired. Your healthy mental state and emotional control is much, much, much more important in trading. I used to think of how my IT job takes away focus from my trading; it was hard. But then, I know I have to have my job to build my capital and it pays for my lifestyle. When I changed my outlook into "how my work can help me trade," it got easier. I recommend that "attitude of gratitude" for what you have and just use it to move toward the direction you want. (This is deep philosophical stuff right here!) You will feel better, and when you feel better, you trade better.

Health and Well-Being

This combination helps with stress management and peak performance. And, of course, it allows you the time to trade. You can't be trading on a sickbed!

Social

A social activity helps with managing stress or gives you a diversion so you are refreshed when you trade. Do associate with positive and inspiring people or those who have successful experiences in investing and trading, you might learn something useful. On that note, be honest that you want to learn from them. They might even be "angel investors" who might trust you with their money if you can prove yourself to be very, very good at trading.

Financial

Tasks that include the budget, bills payment, retirement plans, costs control, and tax planning help you build capital and know how much to risk. These tasks are not exciting, even to me. I have a tip I'd share with you though: When you perform these tasks, you ensure that your finances give you the ability to enjoy life more.

It's like wearing stilettos, at first you'd have to gather the courage. and then you'd find wearing them gives you the "high" (emotionally and literally).

Housekeeping and Organization

Organizing and cleaning up your life enable you to do everything else! And if you've been reading this material for a while, you know that your shopping skills are a treasure trove of trading knowledge. You, genius, you!

I hope that these views start you off with looking at how trading fits your lifestyle. See everything where you can seek synergies or what would work together with trading. Remember multimillionaires like Sean "Diddy" Combs already use this strategy. How hard can it be?!

Chapter 7: Girl Power Trading

The reason why I believe women can be great traders has been revealed, but I've been asked, "How do you do it?" With a young family and three kids under seven, plus an IT job, a friend of mine once said—if she was doing half of what I do —she'd be dead. I cracked "you think I'm still alive?" You bet, it is the spirit that is willing and taking bold steps in high heels.

My good friend, Lucille, recently had her third baby. We worked together in a telecom company ages ago. I did the IT business continuity testing for a megamillion-dollar network rollout where she was the project manager. She's definitely one of the Fierce Kind. Now she's working in a multinational telecom company. While she was on maternity leave, she said that one of her goals when she gets back to work is to study for her personal growth. She added that with her career, young family, and service businesses, she's just wondering how to do it, and thought of me with my studying, trading, writing, IT job, and home life—minus the househelp and family support that she enjoys. (When I went for a holiday, I met her family in a shopping center with an entourage of two nannies and a driver! Ahhhh, take me back in your arms, Manila!) So, it's time to answer the million-dollar question: How to do it?

Bloom, Bloom, Bloom

One of the keys is motivation. Keep yourself motivated and committed to what you're doing. I believe ultimately that what we're doing should help us to be happy; otherwise, why do it? Money can be earned any which way, I realized. I had more energy and enthusiasm for the "work" needed to be done because it helps me to be happy. "Happiness comes as a result of being in our natural state of growth and living up to our fullest potential." I got that little gem from the *Secrets of the Millionaire Mind* by T. Harv Eker.

So I think I can use all my womanly qualities, my well-honed shopping skills, and my affection for shoes in "trading for a living." If you think the same, then bloom, bloom, bloom!

Time Is of the Essence

Study Time Every Time

When I was in college, I had a roommate, Mitzi. Come exams, funny, we meet each other in the hallway half-awake. She burns the night oil and study before she sleeps while I doze off and wake up early to hit the books. I do the same today. I have what I call "deep thinking" hours and "light thinking" hours. This is up to you really.

For deep thinking, I prefer waking up early in the morning to have that extra hour of peace and quiet. I focus on what I need to study/prepare for a trade. When the baby wakes up whenever she wants for milk, I sneak into the PC and study. Then when I feel sleepy, I crawl back to bed, I usually limit working on the PC to an hour so I'm not sleep-deprived (and cranky!). I adjusted this when baby had a more predictable sleeping pattern; I just set the alarm clock.

Then during the day, "light thinking" mode is on. When there are distractions, I just check up stock prices, gather news updates, scribble notes or file documents, and listen to educational audios during quiet time with the baby. I also make use of "waiting time" throughout the day. I have multiple copies of things I study in my bag, car, office, and bring them out when waiting (at the bank, park, doctor's clinic, etc.). I carry around a pen and a small notebook where I write notes—"aha" ideas, questions, strategies, risks, or next steps. I think this is important because this is the result of your own thought process, something you boiled down in your head or what you actually learned, not just read. I think it is important to write notes and what you're planning to trade, you not just reinforce your learning/task, you actually have a backup plan as gadgets get into trouble sometimes.

We live in amazing times and we can do more things like study on the move using smartphones and e-Readers and listen to audio via MP3s. I will be creating resources to make studying easier. Visit my website (www.highheeledtraders.com) to learn more.

A Time for Everything

I give time for the children for most of the day when I'm home. We do some trading activities together like check prices. (I'll tell you more about this later.) I mostly do the chores when there is another adult in the house. For the week, I allocate days as follows:

1) Three days at the office, do some paperwork for the house (Mondays to Wednesdays)

2) Personal growth at Toastmasters Club—Wednesday evenings, twice a month

3) Housekeeping/shopping/errands—Thursdays

4) Volunteering at playgroup—Friday mornings

5) Pampering—Friday afternoons

6) Fun and recreation—Saturdays

7) Worship, rest and organizing for the week—Sundays

When I first got interested and did my trading, I thought devoting endless hours on the computer reading and watching the market would help me succeed. But no! I learned the hard way that performance and psychological condition are affected by all the other things that I am and I need to do. So, slowwwwwll-

Iyyyy, I had to change my lifestyle. All those non-trading activities actually still help me to trade and I am at peace knowing that I take care of my children, household responsibilities, manage stress through fun and relaxation, get nurtured spiritually, and keep myself motivated.

What to Aim for

Things can easily go wrong in the house; with many little accidents, frankly, my human powers also take a break. If I wake up late or any of the children is sick, I just need to be aware that I SHOULD NOT trade a new position that day because I might just get worried and cloud my judgment. If the other adult in my household does not do his share in the housework, I just let it slide, I do it myself if it urgently needs to be done. In all these things, I aim to maintain a relaxed mood or what Ken Long calls the "zero state" for trading. With the zero state, I am not angry or excited, just "clear" to see risks and opportunity.

I imagine myself in an island with soothing skies. Ahhh, isn't that relaxing? Beautiful…beautiful…beautiful…

Boracay Island, Philippines by Rev. Fr. Noel Azupardo

Chapter 8: Traders, Mothers, Models!

When I saw her, I thought I saw my "former" self in her: busy, tired, and a bit frustrated while juggling everything but still holding on to a dream. She's also a mom and we met in a trading seminar. This is one of the things that hit me long before: if ever there was a group of people more fit to trade, it's the mothers of this earth. Why? Because trading is a combination of so many different (sometimes opposing) things and mastering them is hard... and mothers know harrrrrrrrrrrddddddd, and yet, we still do it!

Top Traits

I've insisted that women are natural traders. Let me tell you about the traits of top traders that you will find familiar in mothering roles:

1) Risk awareness. Top traders don't just take on any risk. The winning trades are often low-risk, and this is where mothers' protectiveness can be put to good use—being aware of risks and assess if it is low enough to get into.

2) Flexibility, patience, and action. You'd be familiar with this if you're still herding young children to go somewhere or do something. You need to use a lot of patience and take action when necessary to keep up with schedules and avoid ill temper, on both sides. The same is true with trading; there is a lot of patience required (to let profit grow if moving in favor) before seizing the opportunity if it starts to fall and take profit at that point.

3) Discipline. This is about following the good and the right for a cause, no further explanation needed, I hope!

4) Being prepared. We're always ready in case of any accident or unfortunate event. We bring extra diapers, food, and clothes. (It's about being prepared and going on with the show!) For trading, this is applied in mapping out all that can happen in a trade; knowing what to do if things don't work or surpass targets even before getting into a trade. It is also about being prepared for "contingencies" like if your computer fails or Internet access is down—need to have a back-up plan. Always.

5) Makeovers. This is about transformation. Women seem to have a DNA for sensing when a change is needed for the better or something does not work. Makeovers need not be extreme, but surely a woman is open to trying a change in appearance even as subtle as a new 'do. In trading, this is particularly useful as when you need to change after evaluating your own performance or the system you follow.

Mothering and Trading

Busy, tired, bit frustrated, and juggling everything—I'm past that stage!

When I realized what I really wanted my life to be and how trading fits in, I made adjustments and strived to organize everything to work together. So I can fairly say I'm a more relaxed person, mother, and trader—except on Mondays.

Also, I use a pretty common technique to pursue my trading goals. The male population is reportedly scared by this "M" word, and quite frankly, it is not "fool-proof," but without it, I don't think dinners would be served on time to hungry little stomachs every day. I am talking about "multitasking." What I do is not "extraordinary," but I make it a point that I do a trading-related activity that takes place at the same time as taking care of my kids, the house, or my own well-being.

I found that we can combine three to four activities at a time (yeah, it can get pretty twisted). Here are a few of my activities that you too may be doing already!

1) While playing with my baby in her playpen, I listen to a CD of my trading course as I lie on the floor doing muscle-tightening exercises (abdomen/thigh) or breathing/relaxation exercises.

2) Checking the share price with my children, I get them to type up the stock symbol and read to me the stock price. That way I get to monitor my positions while I engage with my children and reinforce their learning of alphabets, numbers, and reading skills.

3) Going for a walk (usually with my son who wakes up early) or soaking in a scented bath (usually with my eldest daughter), I think about the low-risk trade or strategies I can do next or I listen to a trading CD. So bond with family while you learn something or relax/let go of stress.

4) Walking with the children, we read the gas price along the road and we plot them on a chart when we reach home. We do "connect the dots" of the gas prices over time and this they learned to do on their own: trace the highs and lows in a stock chart.

5) Looking at world maps, kids like playing with Google Earth; some cartoons bring up cultures and countries in their stories. We talk about "economic features" that are interesting to them, why there are a lot of tall buildings, or people's way of life as seen in markets, transportation, etc.—it is quite funny, the amount of questioning that they are capable of!

Multitasking is surely only limited by one's imagination. If you have any ideas on folding in trading activities, help bridge the knowledge with other women traders out there! Please visit http://highheeledtraders.com Readers Share page.

Top Models

In *Forbes* magazine, I like to read about how mega-rich people raise their children so that they too are able to build on their wealth. The magazine ran an article, "Mothers and Leadership Agility," by Ana Dutra:

> Mothers, especially working mothers, have to be both fast on their feet and make sure they are modeling the behaviors they wish their future generations to adopt. For mothers, new challenges and ambiguity are the norm, rather than the exception. Yet, we aim for not only day-to-day results, but also long-term success.

The author may have referred to "raising children" as having "challenges and ambiguity." This also rings true for trading where we aim to profit from opportunities in volatility (up-down movement) or trends that are caused by many factors, including those that are not always clear to us. As in mothering and trading, what helps us to triumph are our rules and self-mastery.

So mothering and trading are, in many ways, the same. My battle cry: mothers make top traders!

Kids Learn Trading, Naturally!

"Metamorphosis!" my almost-five-year-old son said. He is fond of saying this word now ever since he watched the Sesame

Street show about animals that undergo "a BIG change." (Mama is proud of course!) Kids learn like sponges.

I talked about the trading activities I do with them (that's coming from me). You know, to help myself out. It tickles me though that the children ask questions or observe something on their own and then I can give them a start at acquiring knowledge of my trading business. So far, we've talked about:

- **SEASONS.** My six-year-old daughter just asked me why we don't get to eat strawberries anymore. I told her they don't grow that well during cold weather. She agreed, having noticed the leaves fall off from the plants. While in the summer, they grow well, so there are plenty of fruits, and thus, they cost less. This same seasonal concept applies in trading. Oil is my favorite example—say, when the U.S. summer starts out, a lot of people go for driving holidays and the demand is high at this point. It also coincides with the Atlantic side's hurricane season that could cross over to the Gulf of Mexico where much of the U.S. oil is sourced. When hurricanes are strong, blowing into this area, the "supply" can be affected because the oil rigs have to be closed for safety. Oil prices could spike. After the "summer" season, the oil price could drift lower in what is called "shoulder season," when the demand goes down.

- **VALUE.** School lunch is usually a sandwich. I put it in a resealable sandwich bag and ask my daughter for the bag when she comes home. Most days, I'd ask for it and she'd say she forgot. So I explained I need the sandwich bag back so I can still use it for keeping food in the freezer. That way, we are able to get as much value for each bag. They cost about 5 cents each. So to help her understand "value," I told her, "If you bring back the sandwich bag, I can give you the 5 cents so you have your own money." Her eyes sparkled after hearing this, and she's been bringing me back the sandwich bags. There's no doubt she now understands "value." In trading or acquiring investments, value is a good measurement to use; after all, we only want to hold on to something that has "value." So then, if a company's shares are "undervalued," then it is a good BUY for long term, and if shares are "overvalued," then it is time to SELL.

- **TRENDS.** My son wakes up early, sometimes even before I finish my preparations for trading. He sits on my lap and sees me check the stock charts: one year, six months, or three months in duration. This shows movements in the price and he often traces the chart with his head bobbing along—up, down, up, down, up, down. This simple observation is used a lot too for trading where the prices "trend" or move in a certain direction; the trader can then apply a strategy to profit.

A friend of mine has said that my children can be "traders" in a few years. Like any parent, I would be happy and proud of them to follow my (high-heeled) footsteps. They do have other things going on though, like my son loves to sing and my daughter loves to draw. For me, it is enough that I am able to teach them all I know that could help them look into the future with high hopes.

To give them roots and wings.

Part 3: Must-Haves for Trading

I might as well tell you. Here, we will get into more in-depth trading knowledge that I think is useful for you to begin trading. Let me stress that this is what "I think" is useful. What I actually did was breakdown the trading process and plucked out the concepts and functions in use. Kind of what we call in IT land a "function hierarchy model" for those inclined to ask where the hell I get the idea.

I want to make sure that you know that what we've covered so far are all part of the process, and so I hope you read this from the start and didn't miss any previous discussion of concepts.

OK so ... prepare to take the plunge!

Chapter 9: Money Matters

Don't Settle

I learned that when I really want something, I'd just have to find a way to get it. Steve Jobs, billionaire and co-founder of Apple Inc., said so himself: Don't settle. (View the video of his speech from my website http://highheeledtraders.com Book page.)

I am happy that a lot of my friends read my blog, though some say they "don't have money (to lose) for trading" yet. I say, "That's a great start!" I hear, "Are you kidding me?" No. My friends, it takes money to trade, but then, it's when you start putting together the trading fund that you would know if you really want to do it or not. That makes a difference.

When do you know you REALLY WANT to do it? I knew I wanted to do it when I discovered the VALUE it gave me: more free time to do what I love, more time for my kids' precious growing years, and more money for treats (or new shoes). With it, I can build something more and bring me closer to what I really want for my exciting high-heeled future. So think of what you really want and think whether trading can help you get it. Think whether all we've talked about here makes sense to you and make you feel you can do it and that you are willing to do what it takes to trade successfully. When that's decided, it's easier to put together the funds *because you believe in what you'll be doing.*

Think of what you REALLY want. The sky's the limit. Don't settle.

Should You Really "Live below your means"?

I didn't know why until a few months ago "live below your means" seems to be a sound financial idea and everybody seems to be recommending it, but I don't get it. I realized, maybe, the author and I just don't have the same idea of what it means to LIVE.

LIVING is growing, stimulating, flourishing.

LIVING is going beyond.

Living "below" just doesn't seem to fit in all of that. "Below," instead of going up, is staying under, keeping within limits. So how can that remotely be a way "to live"?

LIVING is the wonder of how this day and age came to be— the fruits of peoples' imaginings WAY OUT of their realm of possibilities…and their wallets.

I look back at all the walking in life I've had so far, back when the shoes I was wearing would fall apart after six months or three on rainy seasons. Not only because they were cheap or simply not made to last long, but because the roads I walked early in life were unpaved and would get awfully muddy when the rain comes. My sister reminded me of the countless times we'd have to bring shoes to the repair shop or apply stinky adhesive ourselves and get to school with wet socks. My mom, a teacher, insisted though we go to the best schools that we couldn't afford. I remember bringing promissory notes to school treasurers, which we would eventually pay after my dad secured a loan from work or somewhere.

From there on, I walked in shoes I would give up on wearing before they gave up on me. Then I had the pleasure of wearing shoes I didn't have to pay for. You're right, girl! I got into fashion and beauty, which got me some business sponsors. To be clear, what I'd like to share is that *you have to focus on growing*, and this doesn't have to be limited by your own means.

US President Barack Obama actually did this himself. He echoes this idea in the article by Jenny Liberto "Personal financial advice from Barack Obama" featured in CNNMoney. Together with his wife, First Lady Michelle Obama, they had a total of $125,000 of college loans after graduating from Harvard Law School in 1991. He shares "There is a distinction to be made on spending on things that are going to make you more competitive over the long term, to increase your wealth, and spending on things you'd like to have, that aren't really improving your life over the long term." So let's focus on improving, shall we?

Dividing the Pie

I want to tell you about "money management" principles, "how we divide the pie" (the income). The strategy that makes the most sense to me came from T. Harv Eker, author of *Secrets of the Millionaire Mind*. Trading, being my business, has influenced my preference for this approach. First, how do you manage your money? Harv recommends the following allocation:

- 10%—Financial freedom (for investing)

- 10%—Long-term savings for spending (for retirement)

- 10%—Education

- 10%—Giving

- 10%—Playing (rewarding yourself)

- 50%—Necessities

I like it because the allocations give you the ability to grow, first of all, with funds for education and financial freedom. Then it allows you to feel good about yourself and be rewarded for your efforts with a play account. Giving account allows you to feel plentiful, share, and therefore, receive (from the law of reciprocity). Having said that, I'd be frank and tell you I'm still not following the recommended percentages. Apart from the 10%

long-term savings, I fiddle with the amounts. The way I look at it, it's largely dependent on your personal circumstance.

This is similar to the time I was on maternity leave for a year, when I made it a point to "educate" myself as much as I can. So, education was the priority; after all, how can I invest my money for financial freedom when I don't know what to do? Also, within that year, I had time to go overseas for the advanced trading seminar I wanted, and this was something I couldn't do once I go back to work.

The important point I want to share is having those allocations for necessities, financial freedom (investing), education as well as playing, giving, and saving. These will give you balance and thus aid you when you trade, so please keep that in mind.

Fun with Funds

Moneygami by Hasegawa Yosuke

It's Your Money

"I got my money the old-fashioned way, I inherited it," so said a Forbes billionaire. A lot of them came from families that have been actively building wealth for decades. Hopefully, we get to do the same. Meantime, let's look at ways to gather funds for trading or investing long term:

1) Don't pay tax that you don't have to.

2) Actively contribute to retirement account.

3) Money lying around.

4) Simplify your life.

5) Combine business and pleasure.

Don't Pay Tax You Don't Have To

You probably heard that the single biggest expense in life is taxes. Okay, to be clear, I'm not an accountant; I'm just sharing my experience and so please get professional advice before doing anything. Think—plan your tax affairs to receive the full benefits and entitlements. This requires careful research and planning but well worth the effort.

Plan Your Tax

I remember planning for my second baby and having one year of maternity leave (for permanent employees in Australia). I thought any income I'd receive from work will lessen my entitlement for Family Benefits Tax, so I crunched the numbers and made plans for when the baby should be born (approximately). I finished up at work at the end of the financial year and reaped at least $3,000 in tax savings and family benefits for planning the birth timeline. Okay, that's easy money.

Then late last year, our laptop at home was showing its last gasps of life; it would shut down unexpectedly. It didn't die completely, so we were able to wait until January (when my daughter starts primary school and eligible under the scheme) to purchase a laptop that we can claim in the Educational Tax

Refund scheme of Australian Tax Office. That's a few hundred dollars to add to the kitty.

These specific examples might not be applicable to you. But you may check the tax you're paying and the taxation rules that applies to you. So I am not saying don't pay tax—I'm just saying get the tax benefits you can avail. Nothing happened "differently" in your life. You just made an effort to learn about your tax situation and all the better for it.

Is It Yours or Is It Yours?

Next, let's discuss trading or investing in personal and individual name or company that you own. Note also the factors involved while trading with them.

1) Personal name

     a) Your trading profits will be taxed at your tax bracket or creep up to a higher bracket with BIG profits! (Woooohooooo!)

     b) If you lose money, you can't claim it as a loss against your employment income. That loss will just be carried over to other financial years when you make money from trading.

     c) You can potentially claim self-education deductions like books and seminars against your total income. Consult your accountant.

     d) Here's an advantage. Managing tax affairs is simpler, while you learn to trade, you can start here.

2) Company

     a) Having a company gives you a favorable tax rate. No matter how much money you make, you just pay the company tax rate—it won't go higher.

b) It also separates your trading income from personal income (salary). So if you're collecting family benefits or similar, you can still enjoy your benefits.

c) Another thing is being able to claim the goods and services tax (GST) or similar in other countries. If you are a "person," you are paying this 10% tax (at least) on almost everything, including trading brokerage fees, bank fees, computers, and so forth. With companies, you get it back from the government, per the tax system. Again, check with your accountant for tax rules that may apply to you.

d) For deductions, education expenses that include travel and hotel costs are easier to claim (with other company income able to support the expense). Check with an accountant regarding your situation.

e) The disadvantage is that you have a bit more complex compliance obligations. But then, if you already have a business, this will just be part of managing your tax affairs.

Set up a business structure that can give you more tax advantages so you don't pay the tax you don't have to. Include this in your research and talk to your accountant about what can be done.

Retirement Account

What is good about investing and trading using retirement accounts is that you can use the money to fund investments BEFORE the government takes their share, so there's more for you. And because you don't even see it, you don't spend it. Here are a few points:

- Talk to a financial adviser or accountant. In the United States, there are many kinds of retirement accounts; ask which is appropriate for your situation. In Australia, it's fairly new to manage your own retirement account. I'm excited about it because then I can control the investments and the performance. It can be used to hold assets like shares, ETFs, and others as long as there is no debt.

- If you don't manage your own retirement account, the other option is to check if your company's investment management for employees allows you to invest directly in shares or ETFs.

- For low- to middle-income earners, the Australian government can also contribute to your retirement account up to $1,000, if you contribute AFTER tax. Calculate if you are contributing more BEFORE tax or AFTER with the government co-contribution.

Learn more at http://www.ato.gov.au or your tax agency websites.

That's more money for your sunset years while you get to practice your trading skills *now*.

Money Lying Around

Sell "Stuff"

Usually, these would be your "nonperforming assets" or those that you keep around but don't actually use, don't generate income, or may even cost you money.

- Jewelry

- Holiday home and timeshare

- Appliances (electric guitar, keyboard, second refrigerator, TV, etc.)

- Second car

- Collectibles (coins, dolls, antiques)

An example is when I lost one gold hoop earring and I still have the other one, but I can't wear it now! (Or maybe in a pirate-themed party.) That could be converted to cash. With the high price of gold, silver, and platinum ("precious metals"), jewelry is easy to sell. Locally, you could go to pawnshops or there could be a kiosk in your mall now buying gold jewelry from the public. Remember Mr. T, the "action star" from the eighties? He's now a spokesperson for a gold-buying company in the United States. Yes, gold is that valuable, a secondary market is flourishing even to warrant an endorser from Hollywood!

Get Paid to Shop

You may also want to convert "valuable things" that you don't need to cash. I have a neighbor who goes around to "garage sales" on weekends and buys interesting things like expensive crystal vase, silverware, or china to sell in online auction sites. I think you need have to have a keen interest in this kind of activity for this to work, but know that it can be done. That could be few hundred dollars every month, not bad for a hobby from "shopping."

Expensive Extras

Got an extra refrigerator? Extra TV? Extra car? Sometimes you wouldn't know but the "extras" in your life could be expensive.

Yes, if public transport is not easily accessible, you'd need extra transport. However, if you can instead use a bicycle, and have bicycle lanes where you live, consider doing so. For good health and cost savings (no gas, insurance), this is an alternative worth looking at. There are also ongoing car-sharing schemes, and if you have house guests, there are always car rental companies to call. This eliminates your annual insurance payments and maintenance costs, which can also amount to a few hundreds to thousand dollars on payments that you can save each year.

Shop and Trade

I can plunge right in to aggressive saving strategies that I discovered from the whole new world of bloggers or people sharing information about saving. But first let me share with you my thoughts about it.

1) What I do in my life, my time, and my money should support my trading, which will involve the time, mindset, and balance I need to study and to trade effectively.

2) I invest in my health and well-being; neglecting these will make my life difficult and would turn out to be an even bigger expense later.

3) I invest in life skills and lessons especially for my children.

4) I look for value. I don't judge value by the price, I judge value by the results I'd get.

The Spending Plan

This is also known as the B word. B for *budget*. This word is a little bit depressing, so let's change that to spending! You like that? Spending is more like shopping! Now we're getting somewhere. Seriously, planning your spending allows you to keep as much money, do things efficiently, and save time. This would help you to trade well.

I must also tell you, your spending or shopping habits influence your trading. I had to do some scrimping and saving last year and that kind of carried into how I traded in the market. I was very protective. I thought my stock would just stay where it was and I didn't allow for the possibility that it could surge. Back in the recession, I was more open to finding what would move (sideways, up, or down), so I had more profits even with a fluctuating market. That made me more aware now. So use shopping in trading for both its idea and awareness of how you behave.

Simplify Your Life

Now, to get the funds together, I anchor on "simple living," especially when it comes to household expenses. Here are a few examples:

1) A weekly food menu lets me plan the timing of shopping and control the spending. I have, for example, a baseline budget of $5 per meal (two adults, three children). I ask them what food they want that week and I work around that with the other meals. I could have baked salmon or Thai dish hot and sour prawn soup (tom yum) around $25 per kilo-- the pricier food, together with a less expensive options like roast chicken (whole bird is $7, good for two meals plus sandwich filling).

2) I list items where they can be bought for the best value. Basics of good quality, for example, where diapers cost $14, whereas the comparable quality of a branded one is $40 (that's a lot). We also buy in bulk for a month to save time shopping and lessen the chances of picking up "treats" that add up.

3) Snacks for the children include plain popcorn, fruits, corn kernels, and nuts that we roast ourselves. I don't serve them things like chicken nuggets when they were young, so that solves concern about fat, additives, and salt (plus less energy consumption and carbon footprint). To keep cool in the summer, we've been swapping ice cream with fruit shakes (I freeze excess, slightly damaged fruit in season, which cost less) and shaved ice. The kids enjoy cranking up the shaver and form shapes; what's more, it's just water. No sugar, no fat. We also don't keep soda or cordial in the house. Another favorite is making gelatin desserts; the kids love to

help in making them or using simple molds. We use cookie cutters, which they enjoy using to form shapes. I do allow "extras" sometimes like butter on the popcorn, but this is the exception.

4) Watch appliance use and energy consumption. Because oil and coal raises the price of electricity, I've been much more conscious of appliances such as washing machine and dryer. I'm quite particular with washing clothes so this was a "big" adjustment. I wash less loads now (I used to have nine classifications of clothes for washing and wash every day—he-hehe). I also just hand wash and hang things like sweater and jacket where it says "Dry Clean Only" (except for very few). A friend of mine tipped me about the peak/off-peak charges for electricity, so I've been following that and air/sun drying more. Last winter, we didn't use our heater all that much (lucky our building is well-built with good insulation). This year, we won't be using the heater much. I also usually just stay in the heated children's bedroom when I have to study in the morning. Everybody will just be well wrapped up. Not only do these steps let us save on electricity bill, they also reduce overall environmental impact.

5) Reuse, recycle, and replace. We must all be very aware now of our impact to the environment; I've now been closely watching our use of disposables such as cling wrap, aluminum foil, disposable food containers, and party ware (plastic cups, cutlery, plates). For picnics, we just use sturdy plastics, bring them home again after use, wash them, and reuse them. That lessens our use of disposables. I avoid using cling wrap and instead use covered containers. I found it is also much more convenient to use these containers that I can use for serving food and storing leftovers. I prefer glass containers (i.e., fewer plastics), which are also convenient to use in the microwave when needed. I like to reuse the aluminum foil when I can. But I do recognize this is being mined, so still need to be conscious.

6) Renewables. Do you know how long it takes to replace those things you use especially those you throw away? Answering this question in my mind, I feel, one day, no amount of money could buy what we need. Scary isn't it? Like instead of using aluminum foil, I wish I can just use banana leaves, which is a renewable resource! (Used to wrap food for grilling, and it gives a mouthwatering aroma when cooked.) It made me think of using more plant-based materials or resources, which are relatively easy to grow (or source) and even improve the air we breathe!

Other Money-Saving Tips

- Don't smoke. This is not good for the health or the pocket, as it adds a lot to insurance premiums. The same goes with colored fizzy drinks (save on dental costs, to say the least) and alcohol (liver problems)—these things don't do you good.

- Buy good clothes that are long-wearing. I also tend to buy the children clothes with room for growth. (Ok this is for children's clothes, not a promising idea for adults!)

- Car pool or share a ride to save money on parking and gas.

- Borrow books and DVDs from the library or buy in garage sales where there are plenty and some are even given away.

- Get a discount or deal for everything. Check if you have corporate discounts if you work for a company. Sometimes, all you have to do is ask. Truly, lots of shops even in the malls are open to do this now. If not a discount, a freebie you can use is not bad. Subscribing to stores for deals could be useful, just be strong whenever the word "sale" is used.

- Look for family-friendly facilities. Airlines, restaurants, hotels, and malls usually have something to entertain the children. This saves time for packing as well as for trying out something new (saves you from buying toy/book).

- Keep improving in saving more. Example, instead of takeaway meals ($10), I bought a marinated half-chicken ($5), then I marinated it myself with one of those bottled products ($4), then I did away with the marinade because it was too salty ($3).

I find that the more we get organized, the better we are able to make the most of our energy and time, and this, in a way, affects our use of money! For example, plan the menu so you would know how much to cook for dinner and bring for lunch to work. The daily savings add up!

Words of caution:

- "Couponing." Not all coupons are created equal so compare coupons thoroughly. You need to invest time so you might want to target signing up for those you actually use regularly or when it's planned with known budget and timeline.

- Booking hotels in online hotel sites even with advertised "70% discounts." There's no room for negotiation (for a family with baby, this is mighty important), and once you make a mistake (and can't cancel), kiss your money good bye! I try to book and negotiate with hotels directly first.

You can find many blogs and websites on minimalist lifestyles. My website, http://highheeledtraders.com has a "Links" page you can start with.

Combine Business and Pleasure

With busy careers, having a holiday or rest and recreation has become so important in modern life. I recommend that even if you're so busy working or trying to save, take the time to rest your body and mind. Like, if there's a chance to go out of town for work, I'd take the children so we get to enjoy that time together and save on the airfare and hotel accommodation.

Being so busy, I also allow for eating out. In an effort to save, we don't go as much as before. I allow this because this gives me a break. I don't have to cook, serve, and clean up. If I pay someone to do all that, plus the food itself, how much is that worth? I think eating out can cost even just one third or half of that, why should I not do it? Having had that break, how much more can I do? Consequently, how much more will I be able to earn? I think this goes with paid househelp like cleaners or baby-sitters. I'm conscious of not "doing too much." I have to allow for rest or help so I can be more productive.

We do limit it now and avoid fastfood. We go where the children can learn something, like a Japanese restaurant, Chinese, Vietnamese, Thai, or the fish market (the children are fascinated with the variety there). Recently, we saw how a sushi roll is prepared, and we've been doing that now at home, with lesser costs for "entertainment"—and also handy for parties.

So you know, I think it's not just the price. Let's go for *value*!

First Investments

I've said that it is a great start not to have money to trade at first. Apart from giving you the chance to have a strong belief in what you will do, it will give you time to learn.

I know a few people (me included) who did some research, thought we know everything, started investing (in shares and real estate), and the lost the money. I can't guarantee that will NOT happen to you. But the least I can do is warn you and give you the benefit of my fruitful experience.

It dawned on me that there are really two things where you need money to learn to trade.

1. Educational materials

2. Actual trading and then some

Educational Materials

- The basics. The online broker's website and the stock exchange website have educational materials on trading that are readily available. They include basic topics like what shares are about, together with the strategies, products, and mechanics of trading. All these you can get online for free. They are written factually so they are a good resource.

- Trader's experience. I found though that apart from the basic information and knowledge, you have to know more from great traders who have a wealth of experience from the market. *Market Wizards* and *New Market Wizards* by Jack Schwager come to mind. Learn from insights and experiences. There are also blogs kept by traders. I like the one written by Ken Long, who is also a teacher at the Van Tharp Institute. There are a lot of conflicting and different ideas in trading. Keep checking the "Links" page at http://highheeledtraders.com/?page_id=544 , where I link blogs that may be useful to women traders.

- With the trading process, which I will discuss at length later, I've woven in some psychology and business planning to start you off. We'll get there.

- Financial news websites (online) are also a source of wider market information. Just be careful not to get too carried away by what you read or the headlines. Remember "being right" doesn't necessarily help you make money. (Discussed in "The Need to be Right and Other Myths"). Another thing, markets move so fast at times that what is written can be replaced immediately by another event.

- More advanced trader education about psychology and business planning is also important. I have done Van Tharp Institute's advanced workshops and courses, which helped me a lot. They have free tests and games too. Check their website, www.vantharp.com.

- Subscribe to investment newsletters/newsletters about the market. Examples are *Investment University Daily* from the Oxford Club, *Motley Fool*, etc.

- Meantime, here are some links to educational resources, tutorials, and software on stock exchanges:

    Australian Stock Exchange (ASX): http://www.asx.com.au/resources/shares-education.htm

    New York Stock Exchange (NYSE) Publications: http://www.nyse.com/about/education/1098034584990.html

    Investor Education: http://www.nyse.com/about/education/1022630233386.html

    Singapore Exchange (SGX): http://www.sgx.com/wps/portal/marketplace/mp-en/investor_centre

The Dawn of Actual Trading

One of the biggest mistakes I did was to trade after learning about trading from the regular books and stock exchange websites. So I hope you know now about the other things you need to prepare.

However, after all that "knowledge," and even after "paper trading," you need to allow yourself time and money to learn to trade "actual" money. To tell you the truth, it's different when you put money on the line. Make a mistake, then you will learn. Actual trading will crystallize the lessons. I've been trading for nine years, and I'm still learning up to now.

My challenges: The hardest thing for me to learn or overcome is discipline issues, keeping losses small, and taking profits. These are related to psychology and self-mastery. Some technical knowledge about the market also factors in, but mainly it's those three.

Your challenges: Who knows? You will definitely discover them after some trades. Some components would be the same such as profit-taking and loss, but could show up in a different way. Every trader has different beliefs and background. Marvel at what you will be learning.

And? That means you have to gather funds to cover education expenses, losses that you may incur (think of it as "miscellaneous fees"), and your capital. Nobody told me that when I started! You are way ahead of all other beginners!

Top Five Reasons to Trade

Sometimes I worry about being too honest here. Talking losses, study, and work, even I feel scared sometimes. Well, I tell myself, at least readers know BEFORE starting, which is better than diving in and finding out later. What's the difference? Your bank balance.

I do have a point, right?!

Okay, so let me make it up to you and tell you what excites me about this trading business. What keeps me dreaming about it (like a lovely pair of shoes).

1) Very important to me as a working mom—I can make money without "me." Once I've set it up, I can let the trade move even when I'm out on play dates, work, sleep, or a holiday. Time is very important to me, I am multiplying my income and time by employing money. How? Selling time with call options and investing in shares with dividends.

2) I can make money from nothing. I just use my money to make more money over and over and over—and eventually take out my capital. How? This can be done by keeping in mind the good old concepts of the velocity of money and infinity.

3) I can make money in up, down, and sideways market. Great in these times, as most assets need a rampaging bull market to be profitable—not much of that now! So, how? Get the market condition and strategy right together and you can trade so many opportunities in any market—that's glorious abundance right there.

4) I can be wrong and still be profitable. You know how hard it is to be right, right? The only bad thing with this is you limit your profits. Still, you don't lose money, and for a beginner, this is a big help. How? Use options strategies like covered call and spreading.

5) I can risk small and profit BIG. How? Position sizing will tell you how small you need to risk and keep you trading; options will let you use that to reap big profits.

Oh, did I tell you that you really, really, really need to be good?

Let It Grow!

Money is a precious resource (I can think of much more pleasurable way to lose it!) The above "Top 5 Reasons to Trade" are not only "nice to have," these are also my guiding principles and my way of trading.

Okay, so let's get this right. Once you've got your funds for trading, let it grow. Reinvest whatever profits or money you make from it. Don't touch it, okay? We talked about allocations earlier (in "Fun with Funds" and "Shop and Trade") about needing to put income in different places. Don't include your trading and investing profits there. It's small to begin with, keep it growing in your trading account. This will allow you to grow your account enough that you can increase your position sizing and grow faster with less risk.

Your trading will be much more sustainable. Or reserve it for that once-in-a-blue-moon trade that has got a massive profit potential. (There's a well-known story of George Soros trading against the British pound sterling with $1-billion win. How much do you think he bet on it? A million dollars is probably small.) Save it for those kinds of trades.

Tell yourself (and whoever else is interested in the money you make), you're not touching that money. Not in a million years…or even just five. Let it grow! Let it grow! Let it grow!

Chapter 10: Two Legs to Stand On

Survive and Thrive: Position Sizing

If there is one thing that made me wake up to the fact that I was trading wrong, it's position sizing. I picked this from *Trade Your Way to Financial Freedom* by Dr. Van Tharp, (p.405). He notes that "the concept of position sizing is one of the two key factors you must master if you want success in the market," and for me, staying alive.

Position sizing, as we've discussed in "Learn to Last Financially," answers the question "how much" we are risking per trade.

Let's review:

- This "how much" is NOT the amount you are using to buy your shares, this is the amount you are willing to risk or "lose" per trade.

- You decide on this before doing anything; it must be small enough to keep you trading yet big enough to have a worthwhile profit from an opportunity.

- One to two percent of capital should let you trade comfortably. Position size is expressed as a percentage of your capital.

Let's bring back the previous example from "Learn to Last Financially."

Say, you have $5,000 and you want to preserve 80% of that (your capital or $4,000), you then have $1,000. Of this $1,000, you want to budget for a string of losses (say 10), which will give you $100 to risk in a position. (Fees are excluded here for simplicity, but note it could cost $45 to open the transaction, so $90 to open and close the trade for options.)

$5,000—capital

$4,000—amount to be preserved, at 80% of capital

$1,000—amount to be risked at trading opportunities

10—number of successive losses you are willing to tolerate

$100—the amount you will risk in a position

So $100 is your position size (2% of $5,000)

Two Things to Think Through

As I mentioned earlier, you first need to learn to last in trading—survive. When you've learned enough to stay alive, the next thing is to learn to grow profits—thrive. You should adjust your position sizing to meet these objectives.

I confess, before I knew all about these (and sometimes after I've learned it), I'd vary how much I'd spend on trading based on what I think is my "need" for profits. WRONG! It's a sure way to losing it all. (I should know!) I really didn't have a strategy and I didn't think I needed one. I didn't find this in the broker's educational resources or trading seminars in the early days. Anyway, you might bump onto "money management," but that is just a wee bit related—talking about how to allocate money to what you will buy and so forth. But this is not the case for every trade. It's not the same thing.

Survive: Take Baby Steps

Looking back at that (painful) experience, one of the lessons—apart from not knowing position sizing or a strategy to stay alive for that matter—is that I traded with big amounts (for my capital). I absolutely recommend you trade small as you start. You are just learning at this stage. You might think, "I'm going for it" or "I've got big dreams that I want to achieve," but girl, all that will come later. I also suggest that you should think that you will have a string of losses, and from the example above, use 10 consecutive losses. It can absolutely happen; plan for this so you can keep trading.

So for the first trades, like "baby steps," go slowly, one foot first then the second foot forward. When you first start trading, just open one position on one stock (or whatever you're trading). Monitor and close that first, do not open another trade while that one is in progress. Multiple positions can confuse you. (I sooooooooo know this!) Just keep going along one trade at a time.

You budgeted for 10 losing trades, when you get to half (after 5 trades) and you haven't won anything, I suggest you STOP actual trading; paper trade or practice again. You could still lack some technical knowledge and/or discipline. When you have good results with practice trading (e.g., back to your old capital), resume trading. But remember, you now have less capital. You can elect to stay at 2%, or lessen that to 1%, but that is not likely to be profitable, given your capital. Don't try and recover what you lost with a BIG position. There is no guarantee it will be a winner, and you just might burn a bigger hole.

Now, you might be thinking at this point, what if I still keep losing? I use a covered call options strategy with this position sizing so I don't lose as much and remain in the business. See the section that discusses options, "Keep Your Options Open."

Thrive, Step Up!

Eventually, you will get to the point where you've grown your capital. Think positive! If you are above 40% from the original capital (see our example with $5,000), then you now have $7,000, and that's a good place to increase your risk. I suggest the following adjustments:

1) Increase from overall capital. Say, your $5,000 became $7,000, 2% of that is $140.

2) Increase only from profits. Say, from your $2,000 profit, use 10% ($100) to add to your original position size of $100 (2% of $5,000) for a new position size of $200.

It's up to you what to use. I use the second option just because I'm more comfortable knowing I only spend my profits, while keeping track of the original investment that I may want to take out from this investment and use for another deal later. Remember the concept of infinity?

The increased position size will help you multiply your win. Think instead of the 100 × $1 shares, which you have now doubled, having 200 × $1 shares. With the same effort, you are multiplying your income. Isn't that exciting?! Step up! Step up! Step up!

A Not-So-Technical Technical Analysis

If you're looking for the hot strategy, fancy indicators, and magical entry technique, it's not in this fairy tale! To trade, I just use an easy and effective technical analysis. I told you my five-year-old son can trace the charts, and that's the heart of it.

Technical analysis is based on price. Some traders say they use technical analysis to trade. They interpret the price information in charts with past data that form patterns, indicators, and all that kind of stuff. They say what happened in the past will dictate what will happen in the future. Okay, let's just say, that's possible. That's why I use *some* simple technical analysis. By observing the market though, we can tell that anything can happen. For example, when the tsunami struck Japan, markets fell.

A few days after, good news came out revealing the profits of companies and the markets went back up. Nobody can explain that in absolute terms, not even Dr. Nouriel Roubini, who predicted the Subprime Crisis two years early. For me, there's no need to torture brain cells in understanding stochastics, oscillators and "greeks" for options.

In this chapter, I will show how technical analysis can be used to measure risk and opportunity.

At What Price?

There are different kinds of prices. Just like in shopping, prices change. Something like when high prices are set for very fresh vegetables or low prices when a sale starts (opens), then as the season progress, they mark it down further with a different price at end of season price. So you would see prices quoted at open, close, high, and low.

For example, traders pay attention to these, interpreting as follows:

- If the open price is higher than yesterday's close, then there's an uptrend.

- If the open price is lower than yesterday's close, then there's a downtrend.

The succession of prices moving in the same direction over time is seen together as a trend and may show the future move of the market. The trends can go up, down, or sideways. Note that your trading time frame will limit showing the trend, like a week-long downtrend can actually be a part of a six-month uptrend. So you have to look at different time frames to see the main trend.

Different trading concepts look at trends to see where a profit can be made. We will discuss that later.

What Are You Looking At?

Price is represented in different ways as well, below are some examples:

- A bar chart is basically an upright stick with little "marks" to indicate high, low, and so forth.

- A candlestick is shown as hollow or filled, depending on whether the price went up or down.

- Line graphs "connect the dots" of closing price over time.

Guess which one I use? The simplest one: the line graph. My trading strategy uses the closing price and medium time frame. I do look at the highs and lows, but these are shown in price tables that I check if I want to know the details. The line chart clearly shows the trend, key highs, and lows that I use to spot an opportunity and measure risk. See Figure 2.

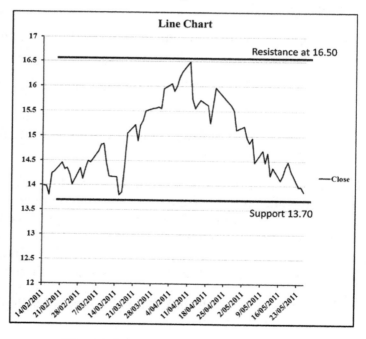

Figure 2: Example of a Line Chart

What to Look for

Look for an opportunity based on price history. There are two price points that can be used to place price in context and where an opportunity may be present. These are the high (resistance) and low (support) levels of the price chart.

Volume, Support, and Resistance

Volume

This indicates the number of people who have placed orders to buy or sell and usually drives the price moves. So look at that too when looking at prices. If few buyers exist and are pushing up the price, it is usually unsustainable. If there are more sellers than buyers, that also indicates something. What do you think? This is the same as when you're in a weekend market and being constantly offered something at a price you don't accept—you can expect the seller to offer you a lower price, right? That usually happens in the financial markets too!

Support

Price level at the bottom part of a range, that a share price usually has difficulty falling below this level, thus acts as a *support* to the current price. Think of it like a wire rack in the kitchen that elevates the food and keeps it from going lower or touching surfaces. In the line graph example above, it is at level 13.83. If the current price is close to the support and breaches it, the price can move lower. High volume of sellers can drive down price past support.

Resistance

Prices at the top part of a range form the *resistance* to the current price. Think of it like a splatter in the kitchen that would keep oil from a frying pan from bursting. (It acts like a lid.) In the example above, it is at 14.98. If the current price is close to resistance and breaches it, the price can move higher. The high volume of buyers drives up price past the resistance.

Your opportunity will be dictated by the trading concept that we will discuss on the trading process in section "Step by Step by Step."

Volatility

You will notice the price either moves up and down or is "volatile." I've discovered that this is a normal feature of the market. You can't expect prices to move in one direction all the time because different people trade in the markets for different reasons: some are value buyers, some are trying to protect their holdings or hedge another asset, or some have different time frames. Like I can go to the weekend vegetable market and buy a kilo of apples. As I'm in a hurry, I don't try to haggle anymore and the seller gives it to me for $4. Then, the next buyer comes, wants to buy everything of what's left, say, 5 kilos, and then asks for a discount. The seller is happy to finish up so can take off $2 from the total price and goes home. Meantime, the neighboring seller notices he's got no more competition, so he jacks up the price. (Isn't shopping fun?!) Okay, so prices go up and down—that's to be expected.

To know how "volatile" or how much a stock moves in a day, get the high price and subtract from it the low price (e.g., 80 cents minus 50 cents, the move for the whole day is 30 cents, even though it just closed from the previous day's closing price by 10 cents). During the day, it went up and down, up and down. Fine.

It's how big the change that you watch out for. I kind of have my low-mid-high classification of volatility based on what I trade. For example, a share worth $14 moves 20 cents, that's low; 30 cents is midlevel, if the move is 50 cents, that's a high volatility. All this is intuitive. I suggest you observe this everyday with the stock you are watching. (You can do some mathematical computations of "moving averages" if you want.) If the volatility is high, I adjust my risk, change strategy, or not trade if the market is too choppy. It's like going on the open seas, you need a stable, big boat to ride the wild waves. Let's say, as beginners, we're just little boats so we'd wait out the rough seas. It's important to know that you don't have to be at the market all the time—if it's not going to be profitable because of the wild swings and your system only works with trends or if you don't have skills to handle them.

There is a volatility indicator called the VIX, which is a symbol for the Chicago Board Options Volatility Index and is known as a "fear gauge." Traders look at this to measure the (U.S.) market's expectation of direction, which also affects the local markets. I'm studying this now to see how it can improve my trading.

Breakout

I'm sure you've had bouts of "breakouts" on your skin during teenage years. This nasty surprise is followed by more nasty surprises. But after a (frustrating) period, they will begin to subside.

Breakouts also happen in trading. We've discussed that at certain times, the volatility would be low. It's just bouncing around and nothing happens; this is called a "consolidation." Then, a move up from the range materializes and you get a breakout! The move can continue in the direction of the price that broke free of the consolidation. It can be another opportunity to trade, so watch out for it along with volume.

Chart Patterns

You might have heard of head and shoulder patterns, flags, or, in the candlestick charting, some cute names like "doji" and "hammer."

Again this is popular with traders who believe that what had happened before is a good basis for the future. I tried to study these before, don't think I didn't try hard. It drove me nuts. But I got so confused, like when does the head start to form? I looked at a six-month chart and I didn't see anything, they all look weird! When do patterns start?

Measuring Risk and Opportunity

In the advanced workshops I've attended, we don't study patterns for prediction. What is emphasized is looking at measuring risk and potential opportunity. Again, refer to the chart in Figure 2.

For example, we believe the market has been going in a sideways direction that will continue for the short term. So we plotted:

Support is around 13.83.

Resistance is at 14.80.

Range is 97 points (the number of points between support and resistance).

Around the first week of June, we saw that we are at the lower end of the range and looking to enter on the next upward trend, around the 7th of June. The share price dipped, then the next day, the price went up again, staying around 14, we believe it confirms the move upward.

To measure the risk, we calculate the points between our desired entry price (14) and the support (13.83), which gives us 17 cents. This is our initial risk (1R). Since we want 3R profit, we're looking for a move bigger than three times our 1R, or 3 × 17 = 51 cents.

To measure the profit potential, we calculate the points between our entry price (14) and the resistance (14.80), which gives us 80 points, greater than 51 points profit target. This is a good trading opportunity to take.

This gives us a trade worth doing that's clearly measured. Totally!

Chapter 11: Basic, Classic, Fantastic, Epic

Basic: A No-Fuss Trading System

In a restaurant, we try new dishes by looking around to see what other people eat. One of those discoveries is pho, a Vietnamese soup of very thin slices of raw beef, topping off oodles of rice noodles, cooked by the steaming hot herb-flavored soup. It usually comes with a separate plate of bean sprouts, basil leaves, and a slice of lemon. We'd munch on the crunchy bean sprouts while waiting for the rest of the food and usually finish with the basil, which leaves a fresh taste in the mouth. (Not sure if the lemon is needed in the soup but it would magically reappear in my kitchen for some other practical uses.) This has been going on for some time when I came across an article that says there is a whole ritual with this separate plate of accompaniments. Anyway, bottomline for me is that the pho dish must have beef, soup, and noodles. It wouldn't be a pho without these three.

Three Numbers Rule!

In the same vein, I discovered that my trading performance went from loser to winner particularly with three numbers, which is the heart of my trading system. I put them together from the discussion of the brilliant book, *Trade Your Way to Financial Freedom*, by Dr. Van Tharp.

• First number is 1

This relates to the STOP in trading—like in life—you need to set limits. Think about alcohol, speed limits, and food intake. I love the STOP because it lets you stay in control of your losses (controlling tendencies put to good use!). In trading, you apply this by setting the maximum amount you are willing to risk. Let's call this our 1R (1 × Risk). I find it best to relate this amount to how much capital you have. Take for instance, your capital is $10,000, and 1% of $10,000 is equal to $100. This amount is not what you will use to buy your investment to trade. It's the amount you're willing to lose. For example, when you buy 300 shares of $5 each, that's equal to $1,500. But you set the "maximum amount you are willing to risk" at $100. Calculate how much you can afford to lose per share with your $100 risk money ($100/300 shares at 33 cents per share). So if the share price moves down in which you lose 33 cents of the $5, you limit your loss and are left with $4.67. Close the trade so you only lose $100. (For simplicity, we exclude the broker's fees from the computation.) You set your STOP at the amount that does not bother you if you lose it but also allows you elbow room for the trade to move in your favor. Once you set this limit, respect it—for each trade. All right, is that too hard? How about making it a habit? For every three trades, you close at your STOP and then give yourself a special treat. (This usually works with the kids.)

I also use this for my position sizing. Yes, most of the time, I enter a trade with my maximum loss, which I can do with the options buying strategies.

- Second number is 3

This relates to ENTRY—*only ever enter a trade if you can make 3 times your money.*

So in the example above, if your 1R is $100, ensure you trade only the opportunity that will give you 3R or $300 profit. That will make you more selective, so you use your money for trades that are profitable enough to cover your costs and that reward you for your efforts and time. This is where women's carefully honed judgement in shopping is most beneficial. In shopping, we do need to take the time and look around. When we do, we are rewarded with a dress or a pair of shoes that are most flattering and that we're able to wear a lot. Any hurried purchase usually disappoints. The same thing applies to trading.

See that? Shopping skills can earn you money—for more shopping! (Yay!)

• Third Number is "4"

For taking profits (or profit-taking exits), it is best to use simple ideas which you then use together.

I use these four exits:

1) **TIME.** Estimate when you think the position will be profitable, this could be in three days, one week, or one month. Otherwise, you might suddenly decide to be a "long-term investor" and stray from your objective or possibly lose more money.

2) **PSYCHOLOGICAL.** When you have a trade open but something in your mind muddles your thinking, take your profits. This could be a relationship issue, moving house, new child, or going on a holiday. Also, when you're on holiday, be on holiday. It pays to relax and have fun. (That seems to be a problem with men but not for women!)

3) **TARGET.** Set a target at which you will close the trade and get profits. A target three times your initial risk (3R) is recommended.

4) **TIGHTEN.** As the market moves in your favor, let the profits run but have a way to tighten your hold on your profit. For example, your 1R is equal to $100 if your trade has "floating profits" of $500 at the highest point, but it started slipping to $450 (10% off the high). Take your profits at this point. You wouldn't want to give away too much profit. This is valuable shopping money we are talking about!

Every trader should have a set of trading rules to follow in every trade. They should fit your unique situation, especially the risk (your 1R) you're willing to take.

Remember the three main ingredients for a winning trade—"1R Stop, 3R Entry, 4 Exits." Rules rules!

Steamy Pho and accompaniments

Classic: Shopping Skills for Top Trading

I was walking towards the mall when the idea that trading is like shopping hit me. At that time, my girlfriends kept asking me to teach them about trading and I was thinking how to make it easy for them. And there it was, "sales" was all over the place, with a lot of women in attendance of course!

Savvy Shopping

I thought so many skills/traits in trading are used in shopping. Things like, we need to decide what we want in shopping = setting objectives in trading.

Here's a list I've come up with:

Shopping Skills	Equivalent to Trading
Deciding on what we want	Setting objectives
Discovering things	Research
Knowing how much to spend	Position sizing
Judging appropriately	Having rules
Making a buying decision (make the most of what we buy that satisfies need)	Entering and exiting rules
Finding value/getting a bargain	Finding where result/value is high, bought at a low price
Deferring big purchases until sales	Waiting for an opportunity
Getting in style (hottttt!)	Spotting a trend
Looking around and trying things	Practice trading or paper trading
Trying new things	Practicing independent mindedness
Walking away if not happy	Avoiding risk
Returning a bought item	Reflecting on transaction
Using credit card to get the opportunity	Borrowing money for leverage

Table 1: Similarities in Shopping and Trading

Shopping Mistakes	Equivalent to Trading
Paying too much	Jumping in too quickly
Being persuaded to buy what you don't really like	Letting yourself be influenced without thorough study
Making wrong purchase	Choosing the incorrect market or not following rules
Taking too long to decide and missing out	Being unable to seize opportunity due to lack of preparation
Going over budget	Letting losses run
Going over budget again and again!	Losing all of your capital

Table 2: Similar Mistakes to Learn

I thought women can use shopping skills in trading to make it easy because *it is a simple thing to do*. You buy something, it goes up in value, and then you sell. Simple. Though I always say "Trading is hard," it's because of the discipline involved. Does this say a lot about me? Don't laugh! You will have your chance to find out!

I bet you can think of some other similarities! I would love to hear you share them with our fellow traders. Feel free to post at "Readers Share!" page in http://highheeledtraders.com

Shopping Strategies and Trading Concepts

At the very start of this book, I presented to you how women shop and the equivalent trading concept. Let's review "Women are Natural Traders."

In Fashion = Trend Following

You like buying what is in fashion and you only go for the *hot new* style. You're in with the trend. In trading, this is called "trend following."

A trend is set when you see most people following it, like wearing the color of the season (yellow green, orange, or ochre seemed to make the rounds in Spring 2011) or designs like the military-inspired outfits. This new thing gets so much press that you really know it has arrived.

How to use in trading:

- Look for the line chart in various time frames (six months, three months, one month, one week). Visually, you can trace the direction of the trend line, whether it's going up or down. Looking back to see the major trend will be one guide, then you want to enter in the direction of the trend. If it breaks through with high volume, then the trend can continue. Like if resistance is pierced, it will move on to new high, or if support is breached, it will move on to new low.

- If market is moving in a narrow range, trend could be changing.

- If the market moves sideways, then there is no clear trend.

Hot trend : Shop and Trade

Bargain Buying = Value Trading

Owing to the global financial crisis, "bargainistas" are shining brightly. It's really cool to see people now paying money for value—looking, looking, looking for that bargain buy. In trading, this is called "value trading."

Bargainistas like to haggle or look for good value, the beautiful, and the functional, without the price tag.

How to use in trading:

- Value trading requires looking for shares trading at a
  deep discount. You need to look into financial data. This
  requires a bit of research about Graham's number or the
  net current asset value (NCAV). You can search online
  for resources or check out Dr. Van Tharp's book, *Safe
  Strategies for Financial Freedom*, which discusses this
  concept with detailed instructions on how to find the
  NCAV.

- Value trading suits a longer time frame, hold/keep the
  stock until the undervalued stock rise in price.

Band Trading/Seasonal

You buy what is not in season because you know it will be
back.

- Buying some popular designs that may not be all the
  rage but they look good and are sure to come back in
  favor (e.g., like bootcut jeans, currently overshadowed
  by "skinny" style).

- Buying out-of-season colors like white or light shades in
  the winter because summer will come along again and
  they will be popular.

How do we use these in trading?

In trading, when you think differently about a trend, that is, it
will not continue or will go sideways; you can use band trading
or seasonal analysis.

Band Trading

I've talked about "rubber band." Observe how the band is stretched, yet it goes back to its stable shape. Examine the line chart and look for opportunity to go against the trend when it shows signs of weakening, usually with lower volatility. For example, a stock normally moves by 1.20. The following day, it moves only 50 cents, then 30 cents, and then finally it moves only 10 cents. You can also look at the support and resistance levels. If the price attempts to go past these levels for a number of days but did not close with a low volume, then the trend is fading. You may also consider negative or cautious sentiment in the market.

Seasonal

You can anticipate a rise in price when the demand is slack; this is easier to observe for energy and agricultural products, in particular. They usually follow the hot, cold, wet, and dry seasons of the year. For example, there is high demand for oil in the summer (due to driving holidays) and winter (for heating). So you would have a "shoulder season" when the demand is lower. There is a build-up to the high demand season so prices can be on the upswing in prices and start to decline before the end of the high demand season.

Online Shopping: Intermarket Analysis + Arbitrage

Online shopping is rocking the world. I do it too at times and tell my friends about it. Why?

- Overseas online websites almost always sell things cheaper than Australia; the difference could be something like 200% to 500%. (I think because of Australia's pricey real estate, cost of finance, and distribution—just my thoughts, nothing official!)

- Plus, we can take advantage of overseas sales on "out-of-season" stuff that we still need (e.g., summer in the Northern Hemisphere, winter Down Under.)

- When the Australian dollar is higher than U.S. dollar, there is a "built-in" discount.

Intermarket analysis involves looking at influences of a move in one market to another. Australia's economy was spared a recession in 2009 largely due to the strong demand of its commodities: iron ore, gold, coal, oil, and gas. These markets perform strongly and are on a major boom due to the need of emerging markets (e.g., China, a favorite customer). The earnings of the government and the different industries grow jobs that enable people to spend confidently and push up the Aussie dollar.

Arbitrage is about exploiting a "loophole" or window of opportunity to profit or benefit. The difference in the seasons and half-yearly sales is certainly a window of opportunity. So, if you're in Australia shopping online from overseas sites, you are in fact doing an intermarket analysis and arbitrage—beauty, mate!

Women and shopping—always good together. Women's use of shopping skills in trading, the world better watch out!

Fantastic: Market Fashions

Markets always change, like fashion, darlings.

There are strong themes that keep coming back and forth in time, sort of like going "retro" with the seventies or sixties style back in vogue every now and then. Or hemlines going up and down and up again. Back in the 1920s, economist George Taylor even coined the "Hemline Index" saying the shorter the skirt, the stronger the economy.

For sure, there are a lot of issues, and I will tackle a few that shake the broad markets and that interest me—stock market, commodities (e.g., oil, gold, silver, metals, agriculture), and forex. These are some of the glaring issues:

1) Debt

2) Demographics: one for the ages

3) Transfer of wealth: new market darlings

4) Climate and environment

5) Geopolitical risks: power to the people

The fashion world seems to have it all covered! Check out the latest trends at a magazine near you!

Debt: I-O-U All!

I wonder if it's the debt issues that rage in many parts of the world that gave inspiration to fashion's trend of color blocking (bold, solid colors mixed together). Think Rubik's cube in a Gucci dress! The trend is seemingly flying the flag colors of the United States, the European Union countries, Dubai, and the governments with the same problem, like there is a "United in Debt We Stand" theme going on. Apart from governments, there are also some credit issues with personal debts (e.g., credit cards, home loans). I guess that's better than waving the white flag of surrender!

This trend will continue due to the massive amount of debt borrowed through the years and lessening ability to pay. From concern about weak government earnings, people's houses actually going on foreclosure, workers have to be let go, and people limit their spending or businesses cannot add staff—not good.

page 146

Color blocking is shocking. (Well, it's fashion! It's meant to stand out!) I suppose these economies need the energy and positive vibes!

Transfer of Wealth: New Market Darlings

All is not that bad in other parts of the world. Before the global financial crisis, Brazil, Russia, India, and China—the BRICs—have been supplying materials, goods, and services to rich countries and have been able to "save for the rainy day" while investing in their growth. It's interesting, following the global financial crisis, the "rich" countries are struggling with their debts and the BRICs are bigger and better. After the global financial crisis, came the new batch of market darlings, now known as the "emerging economies." And some of the rising stars are Colombia, Indonesia, Vietnam, Egypt, Turkey, and South Africa. These countries have low debt and robust economies, with young and big population, coupled with rich natural resources—the *total package*.

With the growing influence of China, Eastern inspiration in fashion is definitely in order. *Asian themes* are gracing the runways: kimonos, Indochine, and traditional prints. After all, China has been "spreading the good stuff" to its neighbors, boosting industries with reduced labor cost in neighboring Vietnam and investment opportunities in resource-rich Indonesia, Australia, other neighboring Southeast Asian countries, and as far as Latin America where mining and agricultural products are the *must-have* acquisitions.

All this newfound wealth translates to rising middle class "shopping sprees" or consumption. This gives jobs to more people who get more money to buy modern conveniences (e.g., microwave, washing machine), which need more resources like iron ore, copper, and oil, so it strings along other countries—Australia, New Zealand, Latin American, and African countries who supply them. I think fashion gives hint of this with *layering* styles and raging *animal/tribal* trends!

Demographics: One for the Ages

It was said that behind the housing crisis is a certain demographic, that is, younger people who tend to borrow. Well, they are young; they haven't been around long enough to save much. That's what they (we!) do.

Now, how about the "baby boomers," the retirees needing money for retirement? It's been said that a lot of their nest egg melted with the global financial crisis that just happened, and any more remaining funds will be withdrawn from mutual funds/ shares moving to cash or more liquid assets. Hopefully, not all together at the same time, but there will be millions retiring *per year* and this may cause waves on the market from transfer of assets.

This could even alter the face of societies. There could potentially be more migration. In another era; people migrate to developed countries to seek greener pastures. With high cost of living and fewer opportunities, many "migrant retirees" think of returning to their homelands. This has already happened even with the younger set of Western-trained Chinese professionals.

Just like in fashion, we should expect economic developments that are *age-appropriate*.

Climate and Environment

In the last few years, more effort has been made to find alternative sources of energy, which is largely due to skyrocketing prices of oil and the environmental impact. We might continue to see these developments in the market, a toast to *fashion-forward* thinking.

For one, global oil demand is on the rise with more people needing electricity to run households and gas for cars. India recently produced the $2,000 car, "Nano," and you can expect that more people will be able to afford and use it worldwide. That's the prospect for pollution and energy consumption. There's so much work ahead of us, I guess *jeans* and *punk* will always be in fashion.

Not just jeans

Another important resource is water. While it's been pushed back from people's minds, the problem is still there. With wealth and development rapidly "urbanizing" communities, water sources don't just get polluted, they even disappear. We can't make water, unfortunately. Fashion seems to campaign for the environment steadily with *flower power* seen on the fairer sex.

Giving birth to these twin problems of high oil prices and water shortage is the rising food prices as well as the skyrocketing prices of agricultural produce like wheat, corn, cotton, and even beef. I hope this lets you think about putting the *spotlight* to the business of trading, if only to protect yourself from these risks. Get ready to *strut* your stuff.

Geopolitical Risks: Power to the People!

Fashion has hung on to *military-inspired*, *gladiator*, and even *edgy* looks lately, probably because there's so much worth fighting for: freedom, democracy, and national security. Early this year, there was a wave of change among governments in the Middle East and more yet to unfold. Some say we're entering a new era of threats: unresolved nuclear issues, terrorism, and even drug-trafficking. Supply disruptions due to governance issues in oil-rich countries also make an appearance in market *runways*.

From time to time, expect global markets to take a shock from this *collection* of risks.

Market Watch

There is obviously a lot to track. How can we do it? I monitor these events from online news. Once a week, I'd read the articles on those themes, then I just scan for any new developments that are major, long-term market trends from factors that are not easy to reverse, like classic elegant looks that never go out of style. I invite you to visit http://highheeledtraders.com for updates on "Market Fashions."

On a daily basis, I find it handy to look at market index for the various markets whether the markets ended higher or lower.

I note the percentage and whether the markets ended higher or lower, if they are green or red. (The U.S. market tends to have more influence on the Australian market probably because that market has already digested the European market news.)

Here are some of the market indices to watch:

- United States: Dow Jones Industrial Average, S&P 500 Index, NASDAQ Composite Index

- European: FTSE 100 Index, Euro STOXX 50 Pr, DAX INDEX

- Asia/Pacific: Nikkei 225, Hang Seng Index, S&P/ASX 200 Index

Another information that I like to look at is the market breadth—this is the summary of the performance of all companies in the sharemarket. You can read about it in the news after a trading session has ended. It's helpful to know whether there were more gainers (companies whose stock price rose) than losers (companies whose stock price fell) and what sectors are performing well. Sectors are the groupings of companies from a particular industry like the banking or finance sectors, energy, retail, etc.

Star Performers

Fashion is such an exciting world because everyone gets to express herself or himself. There's always something new, a twist here and there. If a look makes a strong solid impact, it gets to be the next MAJOR trend, with the media quick to anoint and celebrate it.

In the same way, we pick a strong market sector or issue quite easily—it's all in the news. It gets a lot of volume (participants), and surely, the big money is involved, getting in or out. This is like you hearing about oil or gold hitting new highs in successive days. Before the crisis, there's a lot of news about the biotechnology sector, then due to funding issues, this sector seem to have slowed down.

Another way I track the market is to subscribe to the free newsletter of the Van Tharp Institute. Dr. Van Tharp gives his view of the market in the newsletters. His view is based on the global sector performance from the research of Ken Long of Tortoise Capital Management.

It will be good if you can do the same checking on financial markets from the multiple sources provided above. They are simple *yet effective.* Now that's fierce!

Classic animal prints

Epic: What to Trade—A "Mom's" Guide

So now that we've covered all the concepts that we need to get into trading, one last thing, let's think about what you should trade. Here's a list of things to think about:

1) Opportunity

2) Lifestyle

3) Capital

Opportunity

1) Liquidity/Busy Markets

> I've mentioned that with higher volume, *busy* markets have more opportunities. It's also easier to get profits out quickly and not to discount profits. (I think of it like a restaurant that is always busy because the food is sure to be good!) It is important to trade only markets that are liquid—better if they are in the finance news sites or your exchange's most active lists regularly.

2) Market Moves

a) Up, down, sideways (market type). Can you profit when the market goes up, down, or sideways? This is why options are becoming more and more popular; it has strategies for all those market moves. See the section, "Keep Your Options Open" later.

b) Concept. What you trade must also follow the trading concept that you are using (or shopping strategies we talked about at earlier chapter). See the following examples: oil that follow seasons as well as trends; bank shares that have just been moving in range/follow band trading due to debt issues; gold that is also following a trend due to demand for "safe assets" when the market is swinging wildly.

c) Volatility. This is the up and down move. This is important for the more active/day trader. For example, if you have a stock that only moves five cents a day, then that's not suitable for day trading. I once bought option on a stock that moved 10 cents a day; it took me three months to complete the trade. (Kind of like an experience with a bad hairdresser—not coming back!)

3) Low Risk

a) Low risk, high reward. Certainly, risk is found all over the market, but can you trade with low risk on the market and get high reward? I think this is very important among women and mothers; we don't want to take big risks as we certainly have so many things where we'd rather spend money. As an extension of that, we want to grow our fund (because we have many things to spend money on).

b) Can be wrong, still make money. This is another important criterion for women since we are "new" in this business and we don't like risking big or losing money. It just helps to know that even with mistakes, we can employ strategies in a market that can help us stay on the business, improve our skills, and grow.

Lifestyle Considerations

1) Time frame.

This is about your availability. Will you be able to monitor your trade or be able to complete several trades a day? This is especially important for volatile markets like forex. The stock market is more accommodating to different time frames though some shares trade better than others.

2) Interest and access to information.

This just makes your studying easier and gathering market knowledge more practical. Watch out for the "active movers" in the evening TV news regularly. If you are a migrant or you like to travel, you can use your knowledge about countries, economies, and aiding your study of markets and what to trade. Women as household managers and avid shoppers can certainly tap into knowledge and interest to assess companies that you deal with or patronize (e.g., consumer, utilities companies or bank). Remember: make money from people making money from you.

3) Protection.

Can you use it to protect yourself (hedge) against rising prices? Ever felt helpless with rising price of gas or how fresh food prices have been jumping or with hefty interest repayments to your mortgage? These are avoided by trading markets or shares that can protect or compensate you for the lifestyle costs that keep rising.

How Big Is Your Capital?

1) This is important because the number of units you can trade will achieve profits worth your effort and time.

For example, a share of Google is worth $528, if we have $5,000, you can buy 9 shares. If you buy General Electric (GE) worth $19, with $5,000, you can buy 263 shares. In a month's time Google moves by $10 and multiplied with the 9 shares you hold is equal to $90. On the other hand, GE moves $1.25 and multiplied with the 263 shares you hold is equal to $328. The more suitable stock to trade is GE than Google. I'll take the $328 month profit potential than the $90.

So think whether your month's trading will pay you well for your time, and effort. Will you take this kind of pay when you work for somebody else?

2) Will you be able to satisfy all the financial responsibilities of trading?

Some trading markets need you to take physical delivery, like the commodities gold and oil. So storage or warehouse cost should be part of your funding capability.If you're interested in these commodities but you don't have the capital to trade the commodity, then you can trade shares that produce or somehow involve (like transport) these commodities, ETFs, or derivatives (options).

The margin requirements are also taken into consideration. Margin is just a part of the total sum of money to buy the asset to secure the transaction. Some options strategies also require margin. While it is attractive that only a portion of funds or margin is required to trade, the margin requirements change along with the value of the stock or asset being traded; you need to have enough funds to tolerate such changes in value.

3) Will your capital be large enough to protect you?

Your capital is like a wall- The bigger the wall, the better the protection. This means that your capital needs to be large enough to withstand losses and allow you to keep trading. Also, I will share how I trade using a protective strategy with a covered call. For that, you need to have enough funds to hold enough shares before you can write the options contract that will protect it.

Weighty Questions

That was quite a long list of considerations; certainly, each person would give different importance when selecting a market to trade. Just to help you make a decision, score each one according to how much you think it is important to you, here's an example:

Selection Criteria	Weighting	Shares	Forex
Opportunity			
Liquidity	16	✔	✔
Market moves	20	✔ (with options)	✔
Low risk	**21**	✔ (with options)	✔
Lifestyle			
Time frame (short)	9	✔	✔
Interest	8	✔	✔
Protection	10	✔	✔
Capital (7,000 example)	16	✔	X
TOTAL	100		

Table 3: Scorecard for Markets to Trade

From the above table, it looks like I have to emphasize looking for a market that meets my opportunity criteria, low risk being number 1, followed closely by market moves. I want to have as many opportunities in different markets, then capital and liquidity with equal importance.

I've also provided an example indicating how shares and forex could be evaluated against these criteria. Where I've indicated "with options," you need to employ options strategies on the stock to be able to satisfy that criteria (for example, to lower risk). Still within shares, as mentioned, liquidity can be different.

It is really all up to you what to trade. I only recommend thinking about the above criteria to set a good basis for low-risk high-reward trading.

Chapter 12: Keep Your Options Open

Mango, *rambutan*, durian, *santol*, mangosteen, papaya, *lanzones*, jackfruit, guava, star apple, *duhat* (black plum), *sineguelas*, cashew, *camachile*, *aratiles*, tamarind—I am overdoing the examples. I'm just so excited! These are the tropical fruits of my childhood! Of them all, mangoes are my favorite, just the sight of them—green or ripe— makes my mouth water!

You might have heard from some people that options are risky. But they're just like exotic fruits. Something you are probably unfamiliar with, but when you get a taste and get to know them better, you will like them.

Mmmmmmm Mango by Villamor Bon

Options Basics

I've mentioned options in the earlier chapters; we will discuss it here in detail. We will talk about options on shares that can be traded by the public. These are called "exchange-traded options".

First, a definition: "[An] option is a *contract* between two parties giving the taker (buyer) the right, but not the obligation, either to Buy or Sell a parcel of shares at a specified price on or before a specified date."

Clear as mud? Let's break it down.

1) It is a contract, an agreement; you don't have to own anything to enter into a contract.

2) There are two parties. Think about two people shaking hands; both of them have interests and think they can get what they want when doing the contract. In this case, someone is buying the contract that someone is selling.

   a) The buyer is called a "taker" who takes up the contract.

   b) The seller is called the "writer" who should be willing to satisfy the responsibilities of the contract, *at all times*.

3) To buy a contract gives a "right" but not the obligation. It's probably where it gets its name—it's "optional." The buyer doesn't have to do something she does not want to do. (Like I have the "right to remain silent"—that I don't use much!)

4) The contract is tied to an asset; in the statement above, it's referring to shares. When you exercise your right to buy, for example, *you are buying the asset*, or in this case, the shares at an agreed price (see number 5).

5) The parties to the contract choose to deal with the *price* they want. For example, at $12.50, it is called "exercise price" or "strike price." If the taker wants to exercise her right to buy, she will do so at this price.

6) The contract expires. You choose a contract with the expiration date you want. The transaction can be closed before or on the expiration date. If the buyer doesn't want to exercise her right, the contract will just expire and become worthless. The parties are then freed from the contract.

Here are more information details on options:

7) There is a *price to pay* for this convenience. For the buyer to have this "right," she pays a price called the *premium*, to the seller. The seller keeps this "premium" no matter what happens. This is a sure income for the seller— for this, the *seller is obligated at all times* to deliver what is required in the contract. The premium is quoted per share and paid per contract (see number 8).

8) A contract covers 100 shares (or European style is 1,000), also known as "contract size." The premium payable for the contract is computed as follows:

   i) The premium quoted per share is 15 cents, multiplied by 100 (shares covered by the contract), the total premium to be paid is $15 per contract. Sometimes the contract size varies, but generally, there are 100 shares in a single contract.

9) You identify the contract you want to trade on by the options series, the name given to the contract. This is set by the exchange where you trade and readily identify the following elements:

   • Asset

   • Strike price

   • Expiry date

   • Contract size

The premium is arrived at by the buyer and seller of the contract through their orders that get matched in the market.

For example:

STODW8—when you transact on this series:

- Asset is STO (Santos Oil and Gas Company, symbol is STO)

- Strike price: $14.61

- Expiry date: 25 August 2011

- Contract size: 100

- Premium: 35 cents

Each series is already designated their option type (see number 10).

Each series will have an indication of how many people have open transactions in that series; the term is "open interest," which will indicate how "liquid" it is or how busy. This is one of the things to look at in our low-risk opportunity summary in the trading process.

10) There are two types of options contracts:

a) Call options contract give the taker the "right to buy"

b) Put options contract give the taker the "right to sell"

Here's a summary of rights and obligations for the two types of options:

Taker

Call: the right to buy

Put: the right to sell

Writer

> Call: the obligation to sell

> Put: the obligation to buy

Example:

Call Option

STO's current price in early June is 14.11. STODW8 14.61 Call option gives the taker the right to buy 100 STO shares for 14.61 each, on or before the expiry date of the option in August. Premium paid is 35 cents per share and taker buys 5 contracts of 100 shares, paying the writer $175 (0.35 per share × 5 contracts × 100 shares).

If exercised, the writer of the option must sell 500 shares of STO at $14.61, receiving $7,305 for his shares and keeping the additional $175 received as premium.

If the STO price does not go above $14.61, the writer keeps her shares and the $175 premium, while the taker gets no benefit. *Call option is only profitable ABOVE the strike price.* The option becomes worthless. She can sell the option with profit or loss before it expires or let it lapse.

Put Option

STO's current price is $14.11. STODK8 $14.14 put option gives the taker the right to sell 100 STO shares for $14.14 each, on or before the expiry date of the option in August. The premium paid is 50 cents.

If exercised, the writer of the option *must* buy 500 shares at $14.14, paying $7,070 less the $250 received as premium.

The taker can sell the option perhaps even with profit or loss, before it expires or before it is allowed to lapse. *Put option is only profitable to the buyer BELOW the strike price.*

The Price to Pay

For the "right" granted by the contract, *premium* is paid and has two parts.

1) **Intrinsic Value**. This is the difference between the market price of the underlying share and the exercise price of the option.

   For example, in the put options above, STODK8, the market share price is $14.11, the strike price is $14.14, and the difference of the two prices is 3 cents (the intrinsic value).

2) **Time Value**. This is what remains of the premium, less the intrinsic value.

   In the same example, STODK8, the premium is 50 cents, the intrinsic value is 3 cents, and the time value is 47 cents.

You will notice that for the put option example above, the time value is high, this is because the current price is below the strike price and the series STODK8 expiry is still two months away. It's like saying the option is already profitable; hence, it has a higher value, the term "in the money" applies in this situation.

On the other hand, for the call option example, the current price of $14.11 is below (and is still far from) the strike price of $14.61. It has no intrinsic value, only time value. The term "out of the money" applies.

There are mathematical computations on how options are priced, however in actual trading, prices are simply determined by the buyers and sellers agreeing in the market.

Why Do It?

There is obviously a lot to consider, and for sure, there are risks. Like the "exotic fruits" I was telling you about, there are risks to get them: getting less than ripe or slightly bitter fruit, being bitten by ants, getting scratched, or falling from the tree. Still, we go in search of the ripe and good ones because we know how delicious (and healthy!) they are. It takes practice, perseverance, and experience (some height?) to get to the fruits, so when we were kids, when all else fails, we'd usually ask an older person for help. Well, I got my high heels on, I'm old enough, and I've been trading options from the beginning, and here are the fruits of my experience.

Why should we consider options in our overall investment? A recent Bloomberg article by Jeff Kearns, Nina Mehta "Options Trading Heads for Record Volume as U.S. Institutions Increase Use" discussed a growing trend among investors that indicated options are getting more popular. Given the market featuring a lot of uncertainties, it has become clear that it's hard to get good results with the traditional "buy-and-hold" strategies. Investors demand better returns on their money and protection of the value of their assets. We can look to options strategies that provide ways to satisfy that demand and improve performance.

Be Selective

The first thing I have to admit upon rising from the ashes of my trading debut is that my funds for trading are small to start with and I just can't keep adding to it if I'm losing money. I have growing children, and for sure, their needs are many. We have to prepare for the future. It is certainly unacceptable to lose all of it again. (Sounds so serious!) Anyway, that's what I've tasked myself to do and move forward.

That means I need to make the most of the capital and achieve the following:

- Protect my investment

- Income is produced

- Grow the investment

Remember PRING investing? I've been attending seminars on wealth creation and did several businesses and real estate deals before and was able to boil down the lessons from them and my trading failure. I found a way to fulfill all three by employing ideas that help us to last financially, as discussed earlier: velocity of money (aim to reuse and redeploy it), infinity (aim to fish out your capital quickly and get a return from zero), and position sizing (ensuring we are able to fund series of trades that will meet our goal). These are best-implemented with options strategies on shares I hold.

I only trade what fulfills the "Top 5 Reasons to Trade" (as discussed in the section of the same name), most of them by three options strategies:

1) Writing a covered call option

2) Buying a call option

3) Buying a put option

There are advanced buying strategies like spreads and straddles that can achieve "being wrong and still profitable," but they require two legs of transaction. I'm not including them here (like "forbidden fruits") to keep within our position sizing considerations but it would be good for your perspective to read on such strategies.

Risks: Make It Work for You or Avoid It!

Now let's talk about the risks in trading in options:

1) Options are considered risky because at the most basic buy-only strategies, the value of the option goes down as you get closer to expiry. This is called "time decay."

   What to do: Time decay works against buying strategies, and works in favor of the sell side of an opening transaction. This is best when you already own the shares, done with the covered call strategy.

2) Unlimited loss—while it is true that you have a sure profit, some "naked" selling strategies carry unlimited loss. Naked selling means selling options without the shares like in writing calls or naked put selling.

   What to do: Avoid the strategies where your loss will be unlimited. We can find that buying strategies are easier and safer to use for trading because you know how much you risk at the start and it is limited. The important rule is to *follow position sizing when buying options.*

3) You can be stuck. Remember "liquidity" is your ability to get in and out of the market easily. You might want to get out to limit your loss or take your profit and no one wants to do the other side of the transaction.

   What to do: Avoid shares or options series with low volume. Observe this over time by checking up on the number of buyers and sellers on the series or the open interest; check the active options list in your exchange. Select the stock whose options market has high volume of transactions. Exchanges usually have market makers (professional traders) that can fill trades, but it is safer to be in the liquid stock options series and markets.

4) Some options strategies are expensive to implement. Options fees are much higher already than straight buying and selling of shares, and these strategies involve simultaneous buying and selling or two legs of transactions. This will add to the transaction costs that may eat up your profits.

> **What to do**: Avoid these strategies until you have built up your account. Important rule is to *follow position sizing when buying options.*

> Again, this is like "exotic fruits." For sure, we may not like everything. For me, there are fruits with texture or aftertaste that's not pleasing, just like the pink-bell shaped fruit "makopa" or wax jambu as known in other parts of the world. It is a pretty little thing but I don't think I ever found a sweet one, it also tends to be dry and spongy inside. So since I don't really like them, I don't eat them. I can live blissfully without them. Similarly, with options you can do your trading business without the riskier strategies. Just do the ones you are comfortable with that offer low risk. It's that simple.

Three Low-Risk Options Strategies

Okay, going through those Top 5 Reasons to Trade and the risks that can be encountered in options, I arrived at three low-risk options strategies that make the cut.

Writing Covered Call Option

We said earlier, a taker buys a contract to have "the right to buy." With this strategy, you are the writer selling the contract and are obligated to sell at the strike price and receive the premium. You have to own the shares to be able to do this strategy or purchase the shares and immediately write a call option against it—a buy and write strategy—which is a slight variation but has the same goal of protection.

If the taker expects the price of the stock to go up, you—the writer —expect the price to go down, just up slightly, or don't move much. If you happen to be wrong in your view, say the stock surged, the worst that can happen is you have to sell your shares at the strike price.

Let's use the earlier example on call option:

The STO's current price in early June is $14.11. STODW8 $14.61 call option gives the taker the right to buy 100 STO shares for 14.61 each on or before the expiry date of the option in August. Premium paid is 35 cents per share and taker buys five contracts of 100 shares, paying the writer $175 (35 cents per share × 5 contracts × 100 shares).

The writer may have bought STO at $14 before writing the call option with this strategy; she ensures a profit by selecting the strike price of $14.61 and receiving 35 cents per share.

If the writer is correct in her view and the share price went down or moved up but stayed below the strike price, she can buy back the contract and close out on her responsibilities to it. She is free to write another contract on the *same shares* she is holding.

Price and Profit	Per Share (in $)	If Exercised × 5 Contracts (in $)	If Not Exercised × 5 Contracts (in $)
Purchase price	14.00	7,000.00	
Sold at strike price	14.61	7,305.00	
Premium received	0.35	175.00	175.00
Total profit (strike price less purchase price + premium)	0.96	480.00	175.00
		Per year	175.00 × 12 months = 2,100.00
		% Return	2,100 divided by 7,000.00 = 30%

Table 4: Summary of Results for Covered Call Option

If you gave up your shares, you made $480, which is 6.8% of your capital. You can of course buy shares again and redo the transaction.

If NOT exercised, you earn $175 on the transaction; you can do this every month. So for a year (12 months), you would have earned $2,100, or 30% of your $7,000. Even if you just make half of this amount, that's still 15%.

Let us evaluate this:

Trading Criteria	Writing Covered Call	How
Make money without "me" by selling time	✔	Selling a call option with long expiry that has high time value
Make money from nothing (reuse capital then take out)	✔	You're adding income using your shares with no additional outlay
Make money in up, down, sideways market	✔ up, down, sideways	Yes, you can do this by selecting the strike price. "In-the-money" is best for expecting a down move.
Be wrong and still profitable	✔	Yes, use strike price higher than purchase price. The premium you receive is additional profit.
Risk small and profit BIG (low risk, high reward)	✔	You did not risk anything anymore, you even protected your shares from a fall in value with the premium received

Table 5: Evaluating Covered Call Against Trading Criteria

Buy Call Option

What it is. This strategy allows the buyer to have the "right to buy" and a good strategy to use when expecting prices to go *up*. For this privilege, you pay a premium, which is just a fraction of money (compared with owning shares) that will allow you to profit from a move up in price.

When you are wrong. Say, the stock price fell; the worst that can happen is you lose the premium you paid. It's so important to observe your position-sizing rule.

Let's again use the earlier example on call option:

STO's current price in early June is $14.11. You bought five STODW8 contracts at $14.61 call option, which gives you the right to buy 500 STO shares for $14.61 each, on or before the expiry date of the option in August. The premium paid is 35 cents per share, and buying five contracts of 100 shares pays the premium of $175 (35 cents per share × 5 contracts × 100 shares).

If the price goes up as you expected, you could choose two options:

1) At expiry, buy 500 shares of STO at $14.61, paying $7,305 for the shares and keeping in mind the additional 35 cents per share you paid, or $175. For the strategy to be worthwhile, the price has to be higher than $14.96 (the strike price plus premium paid) as well as the fees you paid.

2) If you don't want to exercise and merely profit from the move up, sell the option. The new premium price will be dependent on the current price and on how much time is left before expiry.

Transaction Details	Per Share (in $)	If Exercising × 5 Contracts (in $)	If Selling Option × 5 Contracts (in $)
A. STODW7 strike price	14.61	7,305.00	
B. Premium paid	0.35	175.00	175.00
C. Share price after a month	15.20	7,601.00	
D. New premium from C	0.59	295.00	295.00
E. Profit from premium (D - B)	0.24	120.00	120.00
F. Breakeven (A + B)	14.96		
G. Percentage profit (E/B)			68.5%
		Per year	120.00 × 12 months = 1,440.00

Table 6: Summary of Results for Buying Call Option

If the STO's price does not go above $14.61, the taker gets no benefit. *Call option is only profitable ABOVE the strike price*. She can also sell the option with profit or loss before it expires or let it lapse.

Buy Put Option

What it is. This strategy allows the buyer to have the "right to sell," and a good strategy to use when expecting prices to go *down*. You do not have to own any shares. When you want to exercise your right to sell, you can buy from the market at a lower price. (You lose money when you exercise your right above the strike price.) For this privilege, you pay a premium, which is just a fraction of money (compared with owning shares) that will allow you to profit from a move *down* in price.

When you are wrong, say, the stock price went up, the worst that can happen is you lose the premium you paid. So it's important to observe your position-sizing rule.

We use the earlier example on put option:

The STO's current price is $14.11. You bought five contracts of STODK8 at $14.14 put option, which gives you the right to sell 500 STO shares for $14.14 each on or before the expiry date of the option in August. The premium paid is 50 cents per share, and buying five contracts of 100 shares, you pay a premium of $250 (50 cents per share × 5 contracts × 100 shares)

If the price goes down as you expected, you could choose two options:

1) At expiry, sell 500 shares of STO at $14.14, selling $7,070 for the shares and keeping in mind the additional 50 cents per share you paid, or $250. For the strategy to be worthwhile, the price has to be lower than $13.64, which is the strike price, less the premium paid. (We're not considering the fees you paid here, but you must do so in real life.)

2) If you don't want to exercise and merely profit from the move down, close the transaction by selling the option. The new premium price will be dependent on the current price and how much time is left before expiry.

Transaction Details	Per Share (in $)	If Exercising × 5 Contracts (in $)	If Selling Option × 5 Contracts (in $)
A. STODK8 strike price	14.14	7,070.00	
B. Premium paid	0.50	250.00	250.00
C. Stock price after a month	13.50	6,750.00	
D. New premium from C	0.79		395.00
E. Profit from premium (D - B)	0.29		145.00
F. Breakeven (A-B)	13.64	6,820.00	
G. Percentage profit			58%
		Per year	145.00 × 12 months = 1,740.00

Table 7: Summary of Results for Buying Put Option

If the STO's price does not go below $14.14, the taker gets no benefit. *Put option is only profitable BELOW the strike price.* She can also sell the option with profit or loss before it expires or let it lapse.

There you have it—strategies to protect and grow your income.

Keep your options open often.

Part 4: Work It!

Finally! We made it to this point where we will discuss all the steps used in trading, forming the trading process from start to finish. I use these trading steps myself, which I have developed over the years from many books, courses and workshops, professional, business and trading experience. While I recommend you do all of it, do what you need to do to trade with consistent success. (Add more to 15 steps?)

At your exchange, broker, or online finance sites (e.g., CNN, Yahoo), you can find resources and tools you would need to trade. Learn how to find price data or charts that are based on their own systems. Some of them would have video tutorials/slideshows on how to use their online systems.

I wrote the instructions in a simple and straightforward manner so you can use it in actual trading. (Let's see if I can do it without once mentioning high heels.) You will need to understand the concepts discussed in previous sections to be able to follow the steps fully, as described here.

Chapter 13: Tried and Tested Trading

Parts of a Trading Process

I break down my trading process into four parts:

1) Preparing. Do the steps daily for preparing to trade and looking for opportunity. It includes deciding whether to continue to trade, and if there is a worthwhile profit to be made. In the example, this target is 3R, or three times more than what you will risk. Say, you will spend $100, you want to make $300 profit. You only trade when you think you can make a profit that big.

   Channel some "supermodel" attitude: "I'm not getting out of bed for less than 10,000 dollars!"

2) Opening. We will consider the trades we can do and choose which one presents the best low-risk and high-reward opportunity, then acting and planning how to close at the desired profit. It also includes steps to document the trade for monitoring and review.

3) Monitoring. Once a trade is open, we need to check on it whether it moves along to the profit target or it breaks stop loss level. Strategies should have been done at the earlier parts and this is where you look for the opportunity to execute them.

4) Closing. We take our profits or take steps to preserve capital at this point and complete records for the trade so we can review our performance at a later time.

15 Steps to Trade

I will explain each of the steps involved in each part of the process. There are 15 detailed steps, labeled 1 to 15, but they're not necessarily done in sequence. I just put numbers to identify them as you will find some steps needing to be repeated in the parts of the process. The 15 steps are:

Step 1: Say a prayer and motivate self

Step 2: Ask self about readiness to trade

Step 3: Update position sizing

Step 4: Gather market knowledge

Step 5: Check the price and summarize opportunity

Step 6: Study trades to open

Step 7: Identify trading position

Step 8: Practice mentally for the trade

Step 9: Open a trade

Step 10: Capture chart and funds

Step 11: Update trading diary

Step 12: Monitor trading position/s

Step 13: Close to stop loss or take profits

Step 14: Update list of open trades

Step 15: Update list of all transactions

Go with the Flowcharts

Part 1: Preparing

These are the steps to use to prepare to trade, with a short-term trading period. I recommend doing this daily.

Step 1: Say a prayer and motivate self.

Step 2: Ask self on readiness to trade.

Step 3: Update position sizing.

Step 4: Gather market knowledge.

Step 5: Check price and opportunity.

Note that there are several decision points that will guide you to proceed with your trading whether you are ready to trade, if you have an active trade going on, and whether there is a big enough reward potential that is worth the risk. After doing all these steps, you may proceed to Part 2: Opening. If you have an active trade, proceed to Part 3: Monitoring.

Figure 3 shows the sequence of steps followed for the trading process done in preparing to trade.

Preparing to Trade*

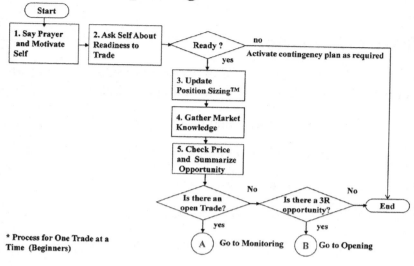

Figure 3 Preparing

Part 2: Opening

These are the steps involved in opening a trade:

Step 6: Study trades to open.

Step 7: Identify trading position.

Step 8: Practice mentally to trade.

Step 9: Open a trade.

Step 10: Capture charts and funds.

Step 11: Update trading diary.

Step 14: Update list of open trades.

Step 15: Update list of all transactions.

In this part of the process, there is a decision point of whether or not you are feeling good about your trade. This includes your preparation and your confidence about what you are about to do. Be very honest here, and if there is a strong feeling that you should not trade, you have to address that first. If proceeding with opening a trade (Step 9), complete the documentation steps (Steps 10, 11, 14, and 15). You may continue with Part 3 (Monitoring) for the day you opened your trade. However, if you are not closing the trade on that day (given that we are on a short-term time frame), you need to go back to the start of the process, Part 1: Preparing for Trading, as the value of your trade and funds may need to be adjusted.

Figure 4 shows the sequence of steps followed for the trading process done in opening a trade.

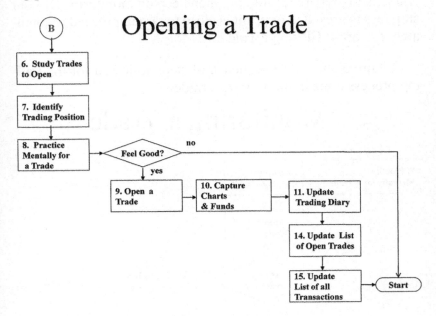

Figure 4 Opening

Part 3: Monitoring

These are the steps to use in monitoring a trade:

Step 8: Practice mentally to trade.

Step 10: Capture charts and funds.

Step 11: Update trading diary.

Step 12: Monitor a trade.

In this part of the process, you are guided with two decision points to proceed with your trading, one is for stopping losses, and another for when your profit target is reached. If the profit target is not reached, you go back to the start of the process, which is to prepare for trading, then keep on monitoring. If your stop loss is breached or profit is close to target, proceed immediately to Part 4: Closing a Trade.

Figure 5 shows the sequence of steps followed for the trading process done in monitoring a trade.

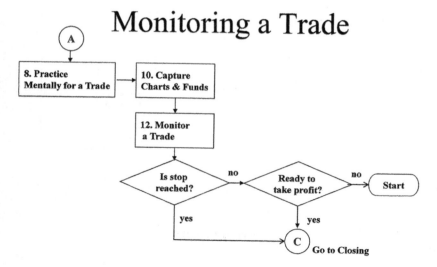

Figure 5 Monitoring

Part 4: Closing

These are the steps to use in closing a trade:

Step 10: Capture charts and funds.

Step 11: Update trading diary.

Step 13: Close trade.

Step 15: Update list of all transactions.

Figure 6 shows the sequence of steps followed for the trading process done in closing a trade.

Closing a Trade

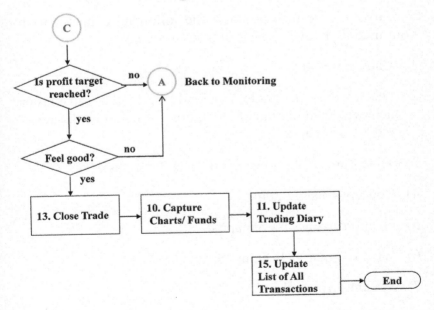

Figure 6 Closing

This part of the process should immediately follow Part 3: Monitoring. There is still a decision point here whether you are feeling confident about what you are about to do. If you are not feeling confident, it is usually because you did not follow the trading procedure and/or system rules, so make sure that you follow all the steps in the process to ensure you prepare well. Action to close the trade should be done without hesitation. After that, follow with the documentation steps.

Ready...Get Set...

Now you would have an idea of the steps to trade in each part of the process. Next, we will go through each step of the trading process.

First, you need to establish the following components for your trading. I have given examples as a guide.

1) Capital – $7,000

2) Objectives - To trade efficiently and with self-mastery, achieving a minimum of 5% return per month while preserving 80% of capital

3) Time frame - Short term (2 days to 2 months)

4) Concept - Band trading

5) Position sizing -2% of capital

6) What to trade - Oil stock, Santos (code: STO)

7) System – your rules:

    a) Entry

        i)   Visual, checking line chart

        ii) Trade opportunity with 3R profit target

iii) Wait for confirmation of expected move

b) Stop—1R is 2%

c) Exits for profit-taking

    i)   3R target

    ii)   Tighten at 20% past target.

    iii)   Also time exit 2 months (this is especially sensitive at the expiry of option)

Example Given: Buy and Sell Shares

In the following steps, I will show you how to do one trade—to buy and sell shares of STO—using the prerequisites (what you need to establish before trading) given above. The examples in each step will show the data for that trade.

My aim is to show you the process that you can use for both share trading and options trading. Although the example is only for trading shares, I will retain the options information for you to have a ready reference for use along with share trading. I will show simple examples using options in the section "Show Me the Honey."

The process can also be used for other assets like commodities and forex, however the information requirements will be different.

Chapter 14: Step by Step by Step

Step 1: Say a Prayer and Motivate Self

1) What is this step?

> This is not about praying that your stock will go up or praying that you will not lose money. Truth is, this wasn't a step I considered as part of trading process; however, over the years, I kept getting distracted, even discouraged. That's when I realized, I need this step to talk to myself and my God about the truest desire of my heart, that I want to achieve with my trading business. Declare what you believe will empower and motivate you, isn't that a good start?

> **This helps to...**

> Keep focused on trading well with discipline to get the results that help you achieve your goals and continue learning and persevering, given the many challenges.

2) What you need to know

> Your dream, life goals and trading objectives, your strengths, what affirms you and give you power, values and beliefs about money that encourage you.

3) Step-by-step instruction

   a) Say a prayer and ask help from God.

   > (*Every morning I wake up/before I put on my makeup/I say a little prayer...*)

I pray upon waking up. Say whatever you want, I mention:

i)   Offering my thoughts, feelings, words, vision, and action so I may fulfill my life's purpose

ii) Ask for help to do my best, focus, use all I've learned, and learn more

iii) Lift up my troubles and problems to entrust myself in God's care

b) Motivate yourself.

What is your dream? What can you do today in trading to make it happen? "I'm going to build a profitable business whether the market is up or down." "I will develop a system that makes money even when I am asleep."

c) Declare beliefs and affirmations to yourself.

Declare supportive ideas about money/success. "I play to win." "I've always achieved what I set out to do." "I work hard *on* my goals and deserve to be rewarded."

What are your good qualities that you bring to this business? What are your strengths? Start with "I am." "I am resilient." "I am capable of producing wealth." "I am learning and getting better at what I do." "I am fierce!"

Step 2: Ask Self about Readiness to Trade

1) What is this step?

   Ask yourself if you are ready to trade. This day, if you have a feeling that you are not ready or you are slow to start, find out why. On the other hand, if you are excited to trade (alarrrmm bells!), find out why.

   This helps to...

   Be aware of what may be stopping you, so you can give it attention and prevent any damage in your trading. If you're too excited too trade, you might take an opportunity that has a poor reward or skip procedure that should lower your risk.

2) What you need to know

   You should be in a zero state to trade—relaxed and clear-headed to see what the market is doing.

3) Step-by-step instruction

   a) Check how you're feeling toward trading today and think of the possible reasons.

      i) If you feel you're not ready because you're afraid of losing money, this may mean you value your security much more than the opportunity. This is normal. Go to "b."

      ii) If you feel excited to trade, think of the reason. Maybe you have a new idea that excites you; however, this has not been tested, and so remind yourself to do the procedure and be disciplined. Go to b.

b) Think of what you can do to be able to trade.

> For example, to get past that fear of losing money, that is, you want to be sure "you know what you're doing." So you need more study, testing, preparation, or better allocation of money (or smaller risk by lessening the amount you trade from $300 to $150, for example).

c) Do the necessary action (what you said in "b") and put that in action.

d) If the action cannot be completed now, then end your trading, resolve issue first. Activate any backup plans if there is an active trade. If issues are resolved, go to Step 3.

Step 3: Update Position Sizing

1) What is this step?

> Position sizing identifies "how much" you're risking for each trade; we will call this 1R.

> **This helps to...**

> Know how much money you have to fund opportunities.

> Identify how much risk you're going to tolerate to keep trading.

> Monitor your profits or losses and whether it's time to adjust.

2) What you need to know

> Know your objectives and system.

3) Step-by-step instruction

   a) Write down your capital and equity –the value of your holdings (shares/options).

   b) Calculate other amounts that are required by your objectives

      i) Decide on percentages how much you want to preserve (e.g., 80% and risk or spend for every trade).

      ii) Calculate the percentages and values that you will spend.

   c) Indicate your rules when you're going to adjust your position sizing.

Information You Need	It Means...	Example (in $)
Original capital	How much money you will use to start	7,000
Current total equity	The cash you have, plus the value of your holdings (shares + option)	7,000
Amount at risk in open position	The amount you have in trades that are still open —this is value of stock+ options you hold. Or your *current total equity* less any uncommitted cash	–
Risk-free capital	Any cash that you have not committed to a trade	7,000
Premium received	The premium you receive when owning shares and writing covered calls—you may use projected amount here like if you are buying stock and then immediately writing covered call on it.	–
New balance with premiums	Your *current total equity* plus any *premium received* from writing covered calls	7,000

Table 8: Position Sizing Information

Information You Need	It means...	Example
Amount to be preserved from the original capital	**What amount you don't want to lose and when the desired amount is reached, you will absolutely stop your trading** **Put percentage (e.g., 70% and then place the dollar amount in the field)**	**80% = $5,600**
Percentage of original capital to be risked	**Amount you will use to fund the trade. Put percentage (e.g., 20% and then place the dollar amount in the field)**	**20% = $1,400**
No. of consecutive losses	**Budget for a string of losses, I suggest using 10 at the start—will let you participate in the market and still limit losses to a small amount.(This is the number of times you lose)**	**10**
1R Position Size	**Percentage of capital you will risk per position, also specify the money amount. As this is a buy and sell with a short time frame, we will keep losses small. You need to adjust this if using buy and hold with a longer time frame.**	**2% of $7,000 =$140**
Losses in R	**All of your losses are expressed in R (e.g., if you have $300 loss, divide it by $140 [your 1R] = 2.14R). Here, we are just starting so this is zero (0).**	**–**
Minimum profit target (5% per month)	**How much money do you intend to make from your system?**	**5% = $350**

Table 9: Preservation Levels

Information You Need	It Means...	Example
When are you lessening your position size (put amount)?	**Based on your capital, when you achieve a certain LOSS level, you will decrease your position size to be able to remain in business and capture more opportunity to trade and profit (example at 85%).**	80%
When are you increasing your position size (put amount)?	**Based on your capital, when you achieve a certain PROFIT level, you will increase your position size to be able to profit more from the opportunity (example at 130%).**	120%
Lessened 1R position size	**Example less 0.5%, so down from 2% to 1.5%**	1.5%
Increased 1R position size	**We will only use our profits to increase our position sizing.** **Recommended strategy: When our account has grown by 20%, we will use 10% of the profits.** **$7,000—original capital** **$1,400—profits, 20% of capital** **10% of profits = $140** **We will add this to 1R at the desired level.** **So, in the example original 1R = $140 plus increased 1R position size $140 = $280, which will be your new 1R**	$280

Table 10: Adjust Position Size

Step 4: Gather Market Knowledge

1) What is this step?

> In this step, you will find out what the market is doing or market type (up, down, sideways)
>
> **This helps to…**
>
> Recognize the market type, and direction it may take.
>
> Identify the opportunities that exist or may develop.
>
> Decide how to take advantage of the opportunities while only taking low risk high-reward trades.

2) What you need to know

   a) What moves the market that you trade in, as discussed in trading concepts, market fashions, technical analysis

   b) The signs that point to opportunity using technical analysis

   c) Your position-sizing strategy

3) Step-by-step instruction

   a) Read news articles/ newsletters on market you're trading. Here's a checklist I have for my oil stock. I just indicate if the news is positive or negative. (If you're new to the market, follow what you read. Afterward, you can update the field that the stock followed or did not follow. Nothing is set in stone, and sometimes "bad news" is "good news," remember?) Also note of critical timelines that may affect the movement of the share price.

   The examples here are from 25 May 2011.

   b) Check market condition and history to form low-risk ideas.

Information You Need	What It Does to the Market	Positive Result	Negative Result
Oil inventories (Wednesday, United States) Supply/demand	Higher stockpiles mean the demand is weak. Higher demand draws more.	Supplies down in the United States	
Interest rates	Rising rates means there is less money on the pocket to spend	Steady interest rates in the US	
Geopolitical/events happening in the world	Can cause supply disruptions, for example MidEast	None	
Weather	Hurricane season in the United States	Starts in June	
Market results (market breadth, market indices)	Check market indices, if up or down from previous session	Had been negative on commodities rise	
U.S. economic news (Jobs, Consumer Confidence, Employment, Durable goods, Services, GDP, Housing)	Some news hint on demand/ market performance of oil;	United States show weakening recovery	
Key Dates- Reports, Expiration Dates, Interest Rate Meetings	Prices could be volatile or move in extremes depending on sentiment	None	

Table 11: Market Information and Results

Information You Need	What is the Opportunity?	Positive	Negative
Price trend	What's the trend?	Upward sideways	
Breakout	If a price level is pierced, it can continue with the move.	None	
Volume	If there are many buyers, the price moves up—more sellers, price goes down.	Low to normal	
Volatility	Low volatility (up and down move) means there is more sureness to where the market is heading.	Low to medium	
Seasonality	Seasonal demand raises prices of oil.	None	
Rise and fall of prices	Prices don't move in one straight pattern; After rising, it could fall with profit taking	looking for further move down	
Value	Is the stock overvalued or undervalued compared with the market or sector.	Slightly above sector	

Table 12: Market and Technical Analysis Information

Step 5: Check the Price and Summarize Opportunity

1) What is this step?

Identify the price of stock and find an opportunity based on its price history or trend and concept you are using.

This helps to...

Measure the risk.

Decide if the opportunity and reward satisfy your rules for taking the risk.

2) What you need to know

The market type and the trend that is in place or may develop based on the trading concept and system

3) Step-by-step instruction

a) Log today's price.

Information you need	Example
Price	14.00
Previous close	13.87
Day's low	13.90
Day's high	14.06
Move up or down	Up
Points	13
Days on current move	1

Table 13: Today's Price

b) Review the historical prices and charts.

You don't need to capture the historical prices, as they are readily available in online sources (your broker, the company website, the exchange, or other finance sites). Though as you begin to trade, it is good to capture prices and charts to aid your learning/review. I recommend putting them in the capture page (Step 10) together with other screenshots. Easy to access and print as well. I capture them here for you to use as reference in our analysis.

Date	Close
25/05/2011	13.87
24/05/2011	13.97
23/05/2011	13.97
20/05/2011	14.30
19/05/2011	14.48
18/05/2011	14.38
17/05/2011	14.20
16/05/2011	14.10
13/05/2011	14.36
12/05/2011	14.20
11/05/2011	14.66
10/05/2011	14.46
9/05/2011	14.71
6/05/2011	14.46
5/05/2011	14.96
4/05/2011	14.86
3/05/2011	14.96
2/05/2011	15.19
29/04/2011	15.12
28/04/2011	15. 51

Table 14: Historical Prices in One Month

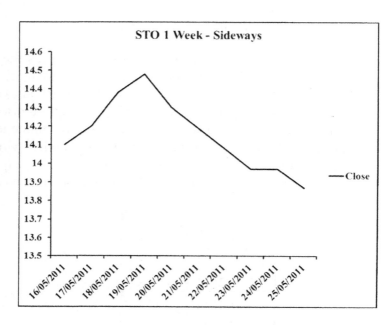

Figure 7: One week chart, STO

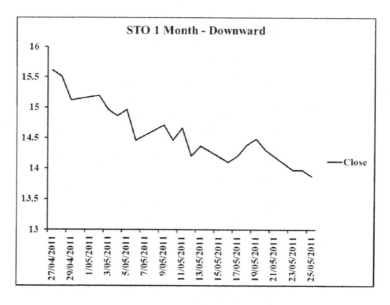

Figure 8: One month chart, STO

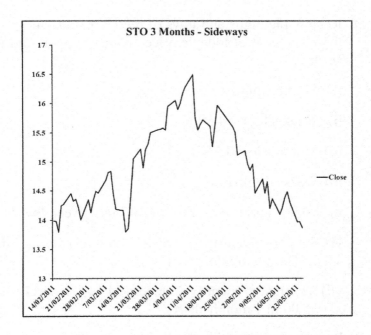

Figure 9: Three months chart, STO

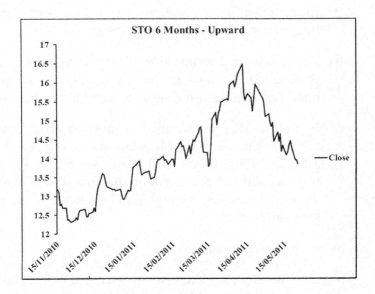

Figure 10: Six months chart, STO

c) Review the highs and lows of recent periods and check the placement of today's price against Support and Resistance

   i)   Month's high-15.51

   ii) Week's high-14.50

   iii) Month's low-13.87

   iv) Week's high-13.87

   v)   Today's price closer to low or high? Week low

   vi) Support, identify 2 levels -13.80—1 week, next 13.50 in 6 months chart

   vii) Resistance, identify 2 levels-14.51—1 week, next 15.00 in 1 month chart

d) Review against the system's entry rules.

   i)   Entry technique - Visual, checking line chart. Draw line on support and resistance levels.

   ii) Do you see a confirmation of the move you're expecting? Had a look at the day opening, was up at open and sustained through the first half of the day

   iii) Is there a 3R opportunity for intended time frame? Measure the 3R based on position size (i.e., if 1R is 100, 3R is 3 × 100 = 300). Since we are looking at buy and sell for short term on this investment, check the range between the high and low to see if the targets can be met.

e) Summarize the opportunity.

   Refer to the previous exercise on price and market condition, Step 4: Gather Market Knowledge

Information You Need	Example
Market type (6 months, 1 month)	Upward, volatile
Prevailing trend (6 months, 1 month)	Upward, volatile
Trading timeline	Short term— 1 to 2 weeks
Market move expected in time frame	Upward, in line with main trend
Volatility (low, medium, and high)	Medium
Opportunity according to concept being used	Band trading concept— market is moving sideways.
What position has 50% probability of making money given the price point, time frame, and concept?	Buy (long position)
What is the risk-reward ratio given your combined analysis?	Major trend is upward on global demand for long term.
ANY negative reason that could make the trade fail or weaken?	Negative sentiment on debt issues in the E.U. and U.S. markets recovery slowing

Table 15: Summary of Opportunity

WHEW, we're done with the hard part!

Just remember that what we have just done is to analyze a possible opportunity. Be aware that anything can happen in the financial markets that will lessen the profitability of the position once we have opened it.

As a beginner, keep only one trade at a time, if you have an open trade, proceed to the monitoring part of the process; go to Step 8: Practice Mentally for a Trade.

Step 6: Study Trades to Open

1) What is this step?

> Here, you look at possible trades given the risks and opportunity.
>
> **This helps to...**
>
> Try different trades you could do, at what price, how many to transact, etc.
>
> Decide the best trade against your set of criteria (low risk, high reward).

2) What you need to know

> System (entry, stop, exits; options—for later)

3) Step-by-step instruction

> a) Write details of the trading position you're considering. (The example here is only for buying and selling shares, but the template I use include options information that you may study for your future use.)
>
> > i)   Stock -STO (ASX)
> >
> > ii) Position -Long, you expect move up
> >
> > iii) Opening transaction - Buy
> >
> > iv) Strategy - Buy and sell
> >
> > v)   (For Options: identify the Option Type and Series)
>
> b) Write details of the stock you are looking at for the position, play/change the amounts, like price you want to buy, number of shares (see Table 16).

i) If planning to transact on options, keep the number to the nearest 100 (because if planning to trade options, the contracts are in multiple of 100 shares).

ii) Once you've selected your trade's details, take note of the *Amount* in placing your order.

iii) In checking trading positions to open, you want to know how you will also close it. This way, you know the full risk of the position, especially the funds you need to commit to complete the transaction.

Date	LSP	No. of Shares	Amount	Profit/Loss	1R/Share	Stop	3R	Profit Target
27-May	$13.95	500	$6,975.00	na	$0.280	$13.67	$0.84	$14.79
27-May	$14.00	500	$7,000.00	na	$0.280	$13.72	$0.84	$14.84
27-May	$14.05	500	$7,025.00	na	$0.280	$13.77	$0.84	$14.89
27-May	$14.10	500	$7,050.00		$0.280	$13.82	$0.84	$14.94

Table 16: Trades Considered

Notes

LSP—Last Sale Price or the price you are considering to open the trade

1R/Share—1R per share is derived from your position size, which is $140 divided by the number of shares you bought, so in this case, $140 divided by 500 shares = 28 cents

3R—your profit target in R, which is three times your R, so in this case, 28 cents times 3 = 84 cents

Profit target—this is your LSP (e.g., $14) plus your 3R target ($0.84) = $14.84

*Options information in the template includes strike, premium, intrinsic value, time value, breakeven, and contracts.

In Table 16, we have several possible trades. Let's go through each one. With our $7,000 capital, we divide this amount by the price of STO stock we are able to buy to arrive at the number of shares.

- Price at $13.95, we can buy 501 shares with our capital.

- Price at $14, we can buy 500 shares with our capital.

- Price at $14.10, we CANNOT buy 500 shares with our capital.

- Price at $14, we CANNOT buy 500 shares with our capital.

Our possible trades are those that are at $14 or below to be able to buy 500 shares. (In this instance, we will just use number of shares to the nearest 100 for other examples to be cited for options strategies.)

Step 7: Identify Trading Position

1) What is this step?

   Prepare the details before you actually enter the order.

   This helps to...

   Ensure order details are correct and allow you to act fast when required.

   Identify the stop points, 1R, and profit targets.

   Cross-check against your system and position sizing.

2) What you need to know

   System, position sizing (for this example)

3) Step-by-step instruction

   a) Write details of the trading position with its risks.

Information You Need	Example
Stock price upon opening position	$13.95
Strategy	Buy and sell
Stock/option series	STO—no option
Strike price	n/a
Opening transaction	Buy to open
Time frame/expiry	1 month
Move projected	0.80—$1
Number of shares (or contracts for options)	500
Premium per contract	n/a
1R stop	$140 for 500 shares, $0.28 per share
Breakeven price	$13.95, excluding fees
Worst-case scenario	Sell stocks at loss, should keep within 1R $13.95 - $0.28 = $13.67
Does my position follow position sizing to control my overall risk?	Yes
Will the position give a risk-reward ratio of 3R, per my system?	Yes
What price should be reached to get a 3R profit?	3R = $0.28×3 = $0.84 Plus price of share $14 3R target share price = $14.84

Table 17: Details of Trading Position

b) If not satisfying the above questions, end.

If yes, proceed to "c."

c) Organize funds

    i) Verify that you have funds to carry out the transaction (open + close).

    ii) Update the position-sizing page given the new trade you are opening (projected amounts).

    iii) Capture screenshot of funds before you trade and put in Step 10.

d) Write details of the order, as spoken (in case you have to talk to broker/representative):

Transaction (Buy) + Number of Shares + Share Code + Price

Example: Buy 500 shares of STO at $13.95.

NOTE: Write this down in your notebook, as a backup and to remind you about the trade.

Step 8: Practice Mentally for a Trade

1) What is this step?

> Top performers, athletes, traders, and salespersons practice mental preparation. It pays to know what could happen and how you want to execute your plan given the risks and opportunities.

> Picture this: You're tired, and when you see a stock move favorably, you're a little bit excited, you see the opportunity, and you might jump in without following the procedure. With correct mental preparation, you remind yourself of points on how to execute your trade so that you don't make a mistake by not following the rules.

> **This helps to...**

> Keep you focused on following your system rules.

> Put yourself in the right frame of mind so that you're not carried away by what may be in the market, you won't act on your excitement.

2) What you need to know

   a) Be aware of the market type and how it develops so you have an idea how to react. Review some technical analysis that can be helpful (e.g., retracement, breakouts).

   b) You need to state your action plan and what you may feel in a supportive way so it does not "negatively affect" your trading. You need to be careful in your language and attitude toward the market. (Remember the shopping lessons: if you're saving aggressively, your view of the market is also that it is "limited.")

3) Step-by-step instruction

> Write your thoughts for mental rehearsal for the transaction you are about to do. For example—Entry: "The market has been on a seesaw lately. I will continue to monitor the market for opportunities. I will wait for a confirmation of the move I expect and maintain self-control."
>
> You will also be using this step in monitoring and closing. It is a good idea to remind yourself of your system rules, to be relaxed and to be in "zero state."

Step 9: Open a Trade

1) What is this step?

> Place your transaction at this point and fully commit to the trade.
>
> **This helps to...**
>
> Check your commitment to the trade before placing the order.
>
> Get the exact order details right and prepare for entering the transaction.
>
> Verify the transaction completed so you may still correct an error.
>
> Document the transaction.

2) What you need to know

> Mechanics of placing order with your broker.

3) Step-by-step instruction

   a) Check your commitment.

   > i) Did you fully prepare for this trade by following all the steps in the process?
   >
   > ii) Are you confident that the trade is worth the risk, that is, it meets your 3R profit target?
   >
   > If your answer is "no" to any question, then stop. Go back to start of preparing to trade now (Step 1).
   >
   > If you say "yes" to both questions, then take action.

b) Action. Enter an order, per the details in Step 7.

  Example: Buy 500 shares of STO at $13.95.

c) Estimate the amount you need to commit. (Usually, an online broker will provide an estimate on your order entry screen.) Confirm this as the amount you plan to spend as you've done in "Step 6: Study Trades to Open."

d) Check the order completed; if your broker offers a confirmation email or SMS, check that.

  i) Check that the order is correct. Buy to open, per our example.

  ii) Check other details of the order (e.g., price, quantity, series). Sometimes the price might be different to what we want it to be if we've placed an original order and we've been changing it. Update your records of the price when order is completed.

  iii) Confirm whether the funds movement is correct. Note that the trading total includes fees.

e) Document and save the trade transaction file (worksheet) in softcopy.

  Here's a filename format you may follow:

  i) Share and Day and Month of transaction (STO-04JUL) or option series name (STOVR7),

  ii) Transaction – "O" for open

  iii) Counter - 1—as you might trade the same series more than once.

  Note the filename and folder location. Example: C:\ Trades\STOVR7_O_1.xls

Plunge In! By Rev. Fr. Noel Azupardo

Step 10: Capture Charts and Funds

1) What is this step?

> You document the trade by:
>
> Capturing charts when you open the trade and when monitoring
>
> Opening funds position (how much you have before the transaction)
>
> Capturing the funds when transaction is completed
>
> **This helps to...**
>
> Check back on the opportunity you saw for further learning (you could have done a different trade).
>
> Trace the funds movement and that the money is what it should be. This is important especially if you have several trades going on; check that all the money is accounted.

2) What you need to know

> None for this step.

3) Step-by-step instruction

    a) Capture the price chart from Step 5 (check prices).

    b) Capture funds balance before open from Step 3 (position sizing).

    c) Capture funds after open transaction is completed from Step 9 (open a trade).

    d) Capture price charts from monitoring from Step 12 (check prices).

    e) Capture settlement funds from Step 13 (closing).

Step 11: Update Trading Diary

1) What is this step?

> You write down your feelings and thoughts about the trade as it progresses (open, monitoring, close). You check that you're following your system and other rules.

> **This helps to...**

> Improve performance later from spotting mistakes or emotional weakness/strength you have written.

> Look at the woman in the mirror! (Thanks, Michael!)

2) What you need to know

> Yourself, system

3) Step-by-step instruction

   a) Did I follow trading process to prepare and open the trade? YES.

   b) Did I follow my system rules? Indicate the values that satisfy them.

      i) Entry – Confirmation (Yes) and position size (Yes)

      ii) Stop – 1R = 0.28

      iii) Exit – Stop is 13.67 and Profit target is 14.84

   c) Note also any feelings as the trade progressed so you know how to manage it. Some examples:

Before opening:

"Was so excited and tried to relax while waiting for start of session. Busied myself with the children to dissociate myself and get the excitement down."

After opening:

"Was watching the market move up in front of my preferred price, was tempted to jump in but thought I could wait around lunchtime for the market to come back to my price point. I dissociated myself from the trade by doing housework and entered a limit trade at my price point, which was taken eventually before closing up to a higher price."

Step 12: Monitor Trading Position/s

1) What is this step?

> Check how the trade is going. Just monitor the prices, wait for your exits to abort or take profits.
>
> **This helps to...**
>
> Reap the reward from your trade or limit your loss.

2) What you need to know

> All the strategy needed to be done ahead of time, which we did from Steps 3 to 6.

3) Step-by-step instruction

   a) Update the values for your system rules in this page

      i) Reason for entry: long-term demand and price cycle moving upward in short term

      ii) System rules

         (a) STOP—1R = $0.28, the stock price is $13.72

         (b) EXITS

            (i) Time frame—one month

            (ii) Psychological —high stress situation develop, apply contingency or abort

            (iii) 3R profit target = $0.84, $14.84 stock price

            (iv) Tighten profit = 10% past the profit target if the stock is moving rapidly

b) Capture the stock/option prices from the stock exchange website, daily.

You may want to save it in a separate file to put together data for price history and future testing. You may want to capture the price chart (this is available in broker website but it is helpful to put it with the trading file in Step10 for performance review).

c) Update the information table on your trade.

   i)   First put the open order (same one we used in Step 6 to consider trade for open), with additional fields on profit-taking exits and monitoring information.

   ii) Then update *daily* with the price changes that you captured from "b" above.

Example: Daily/Regular Monitoring

It would be best if you can update this table with the prices and review the exits and monitoring questions daily. Support and resistance can be taken from Step 5: Check the Price. Following the trade we opened, the price of STO moved up and reached 14.76 for one week. At this point we are thinking of taking our profits.

For convenience, have a list of Open trades in view at your workstation. Refer to Step 14.

| Trade Details | | | | | Exits - Profit / Stop | | | | | Monitoring Information | | | |
Date	Shares	LSP	No. of Shares	Amount	Profit / Loss	1R Stop	3R	Profit Target	Tighten Point	Support	Resistance	Trade Ok	Reason for Entry still valid?
27-May	STO	$14.00	500	$7,000.00	na	$0.28	$0.84	$14.84		$13.80	$14.51	ok	yes
30-May	STO	$14.50	500	$7,250.00	$250.00	$0.28	$0.84	$14.84		$13.80	$14.51	ok	yes
31-May	STO	$14.76	500	$7,380.00	$380.00	$0.28	$0.84	$14.84		$13.80	$15.00	ok	yes
1-Jun	STO	$14.82	500	$7,410.00	$410.00	$0.28	$0.84	$14.84		$13.80	$15.00	ok	yes

Table18: Information Needed for Monitoring Trading Position

Step 13: Close Trade

1) What is this step?

> You're taking profits or aborting the trade. This ends the trading transaction.

2) What you need to know

> Your system.

3) Step-by-step instruction

> a) Collect the data from Step 12 (monitoring).
>
> b) Review the exits we outlined in Step 12. Monitor Trading Positions
>
>> i) Is the stop breached? No.
>>
>> ii) Is the profit target reached? Yes.
>
> c) Check that you have sufficient funds to trade; we've done this repeatedly in Step 3 (position sizing) and Step 7 (identify position).
>
> d) Check your commitment. "Do you feel good about what you are going to do?"
>
>> i) Did you follow the process and criteria to close this trade? Did you complete all steps?
>>
>> ii) Does the trade satisfy the criteria? Example, is the stop breached? Does it meet the profit target? If taking profit before target is reached, is the market changing that justifies taking profit early?
>>
>> If the answer is "no" to any question, then stop. Go back to Step 12: Monitoring.

If the answer is "yes" to the questions, then take action.

e)   Action. Enter the order details.

Example: *Sell 500 shares of STO at $14.85.*

f)   Estimate the amount you need to commit. (The online broker usually provides an estimate.)

g)   Check the completed order. If your broker offers a confirmation email or SMS, check that.

   i)   Check that the order is *sell*, per our example.

   ii) Check other details of the order (e.g., price, quantity, series is correct). Sometimes the price might be different to what we want it to be if we placed an original order and had been changing it. Update your records of the price when the order is completed.

   iii) Confirm if the funds movement is correct. Note that the trading total includes fees.

h)   Document and save the trade transaction file (worksheet) in softcopy.

Here's a filename format you may follow:

   i)   Share and Day and Month of transaction (STO-04JUL) or option series name (STOVR7),

   ii) Transaction – "C" for close

   iii) Counter - 1—as you might trade the same series more than once.

Note the filename and folder location. Example: C:\ Trades\STOVR7_C_1.xls

Step 14: Update List of Open Trades

1) What is this step?

Document your open transactions. This is a continuing list and must be kept up to date with each new transaction. We do this to monitor updates on the go. This is important to enable us to trade despite our busy lifestyle.

This helps to...

Get easy reference and awareness of stops and profit targets.

Know multiple positions that may be in the same direction. You don't want to add to same position if the earlier ones are not profitable. Only add positions in the same direction if earlier ones are profitable and the 3R reward potential is there.

2) What you need to know

Your system.

3) Step-by-step instruction

a) Copy the information in Step 12: Monitoring, particularly the trade details and exits.

Print and post in your workstation or where you can easily see it while going about chores in the house and easily accessible when you need to close your trade.

Step 15: Update List of All Transactions

1) What is this step?

> Documenting all transactions in open and close "matchout" format.
>
> **This helps to...**
>
> See the profits and loss from transactions.
>
> Document and measure your performance for review and improvement later.
>
> Document accounting and tax-related information (e.g., Expenses, GST payable).

2) What you need to know

   a) Performance review. At this stage after trading, you want to start gathering data on how you measure up to objectives. You can use the following checklist:

   i) Are you consistently achieving your monthly targets?

   ii) How many times are you putting on winning trades?

   iii) How large are your wins?

3) Step-by-step instruction

   a) Copy and paste the details of the open transaction (from Step 12 on monitoring).

   b) Copy and paste the details of the closing transaction from Step 12, right under it. If trading multiple positions, sort and order according to the series or matchout, not the trade date.

c) Update for both entries the full expenses information.

d) Update the profit and loss.

    i) Profit/loss—proceeds of your open and close transactions

    ii) Net of tax—amount remaining when you take off tax payable (e.g., 30%) on gross profits

    I find that computing tax and only adding the "net of tax" amount to your position size helps me from the psychological burden of paying taxes, especially if I need to spend profits on business expenses, training, or lifestyle.

e) Update the performance review fields.

    i) Win—update this with "1" to represent win, "0" for loss (just to see your win rate as a basic measure of performance)

    ii) R-multiple—the result of your trading based on your initial risk (1R). Divide the amount profit/loss by 1R in your position sizing; we're targeting 3R profit. Did you reach your target?

    iii) Month result—we stated in position sizing minimum profit target. Target achieved or not?

TRADE DETAILS

Ref. No	Trade Date	Series	MatchOut	Price	Shares	Buy/Sell	Amount
B89764	27-May	STO	AA	$14.00	500	Buy	$7,000.00
C46335	1-Jun	STO	AA	$14.85	500	Sell	$7,425.00

EARNINGS AND TAX- RELATED DETAILS

									PERFORMANCE REVIEW		
ACH*	Brokerage	GST	Brokerage exc GST	Total fees inc GST	Total fees ex GST	Net Proceeds	Profit/Loss	Net of Tax(30%)	WIN = 1	R-Multiple	Result/Month
$0.00	$20.00	$1.82	$18.18	$20.00	$0.00	$20.00	na	na	na	na	na
$0.00	$20.00	$1.82	$18.18	$20.00	$0.00	$20.00	$425.00	$297.50	1	3.04	Target reached

Table 19: Trading Transactions List

Notes:

ACH—fees charged by Australian Clearing House for options trades

GST—Goods and Services Tax, which may need to be reported to the government (dependent on account/ tax structure you use)

Ref. No.—your broker-assigned reference number

Matchout—you can assign a code or ID to indicate which trades are the matching trades to open and close, for example, I use AA for the two matching transactions, then AB for the next trades

Chapter 15: Show Me the Honey

It's not a typo. I really meant to put the "h" instead of the "m". "Honey" not "money". With this I just want to stress that whatever you get from trading is a product of many small steps and you really got to "work it". But the results will be sweet.

In the 15-step trading process, I showed you how to buy and sell shares. Going back to the objective I've set out for myself about protecting capital (getting an income and growing that capital), we have to apply the principles of velocity of money, infinity, and position sizing. We will implement these principles with options strategies, as explained in two parts: Part 1: Buying Stock to Let It Grow and Part 2: Protecting Value and Getting Income.

Part 1: Buying Stock to Let It Grow

Instead of selling the shares as shown in the step-by-step process, we will hold on to the shares to let it grow further. We will use a 1R stop that will give the shares room to move in the time frame we want. It is important that our stop is wide enough to accommodate the market fluctuations we can expect in this period. With our 500 shares, we assign a 20% stop to give it room to grow while limiting our risk. Thus, we need to update the following details:

1) 1R = 20% of $7,000 capital or $1,400 or $2.80 per share

2) Stop amount = $5,600 value of stock or $11.15 per share

3) 3R target = 3 × $2.80, which is $8.40

We will monitor the stock and look for entry point, instead of selling/closing the trade by taking profits at the high price of $14.76 from the earlier example. We will enter a protective strategy to lock in profits as well as profit on the move down.

Part 2: Protecting Value and Getting Income

Remember that this part is done when you already have a position, and followed the preparing and monitoring part of the process.

For all strategies that we will apply, we will keep to our trading system and position sizing rules as the following:

1) **Entry**

   a) Visual, checking line chart

   b) Trade opportunity with 3R profit target

   c) Wait for confirmation of expected move

2) **Stop (1R)**

   For all buying strategies, I like to enter within the maximum stop, so the stop is the same as 1R 2% of $7,000 capital, or $140 per trade.

3) **Exit**

   a) 3R target = $140 × 3 is $420

   b) Tighten at 20% past target

   c) Also time exit two months (this is especially sensitive at expiry of option)

Profit From Move Down

As we have observed, the price of STO had gone up steadily, we think that with the market type going sideways, increasingly volatile and with the Greek debt crisis becoming more pronounced, we would protect its value and profit from move down with two strategies:

- Covered call

- Buying put

Covered Call A

This strategy is called "covered call" because we already hold the shares against which we are selling call options. At $14.82, after the stock closed up the previous day by only 6points (low volatility) and with a move confirming our belief that the next move is down, we open a new transaction writing call options.

To start the transaction, we will sell to open, STOCM8 $14.61 July call. We are giving someone else the right to buy our 500 shares at the "strike price" of $14.61; this contract will expire in two months. To have this right, the other party (called the "taker") will pay 69 cents per share (called the "premium"), which we keep no matter what happens and whose time value (54 cents) will allow us to keep some profit even if we are wrong in our analysis and the price moves up. We choose this option as it offers low risk of being exercised (our stock being taken away from us).

The taker believes the stock will move up strongly in two months; however, it will only be profitable above $15.30 (the strike price of $14.61 and the 69-cent premium spent for the options contract). For the five contracts, we receive a total of $345 (fees are excluded for simplicity).

We satisfy our position sizing rule, using 28 cents per share or the $140 divided by 500 shares, which we will consider as part of the time value from the premium protecting us in the trade.

Buying Put A

With our belief that the price will move down, we will also buy put options. We will keep to our position sizing and only use $140. At $14.76, we will buy a put that will grow in value but will need to be profitable in the short term, which is still realistic given the price history. We will buy STODK7 $14.00 JUN PUT. We shell out 9.5 cents per share. With $140, we can get 14 contracts, which cover 1,400 shares.

Our profit target is 30 cents when the share price reaches $14. (There is a tool available at the exchange website for "theoretical price value" or estimate of the value of option at a given price). As the taker, we believe the stock will move down strongly in one month; however, will only be profitable below $13.905 (the strike price of $14 and the 9.5-cent premium spent for the options contract).

Locking in Profits

The price moves down as expected, by middle of the month, the price falls to $14. At this price level, and with the increasing uncertainty, we are not sure of the next price move. We decide to lock in some of our profit on the covered call but continue to monitor the put option. The first put option we bought for 9.5 cents is now worth 31.5 cents. We decide to keep it and tighten our stop in case the move reverses. Our new stop is 25 cents, or 20% from the highest price.

Buy Back to Close Covered Call A

At $14, the call option STOCM8 $14.61 July call we sold for 69 cents is now worth 24 cents. To end the transaction, we buy to close the option at 24 cents, paying $120. Remember we sold it for $345 so our profit is $225.

Protect/Hedging

We noted the market uncertainty prevailing with the Greek debt crisis, so at the $14 level, we enter new positions to protect the value of our stock but still profit from a move up.

Covered Call B

To start the transaction, we will sell to open, STOCK8 $13.67 July call—we are giving someone else the right (but not the obligation) to buy our 500 shares at the "strike price" of $13.67, and this contract will expire in two months. To have this right, the other party (the taker) will pay 65.5 cents per share (the premium), which we keep no matter what happens, and whose time value (33 cents) will allow us to keep some profit even if we are wrong in our analysis and the price moves up. We choose this in-the-money call option because of the negative sentiment in the market. We counter this aggressive position by buying a call option, which will be explained below.

The taker believes the stock will move up strongly in two months; however, it will only be profitable above $14.32 (the strike price of $13.67 and the 65-cent premium spent for the options contract). For the five contracts, we receive a total of $327.50 (fees are excluded for simplicity).

We satisfy our position sizing rule using 28 cents per share or the $140 divided by 500 shares that we will consider as part of the time value from the premium protecting us in the trade.

Buying a Call

With our belief that the price may also move up, we will also buy call options, which will compensate us for loss if our covered call B is unprofitable. We will keep to our position sizing and only use $140. At $14, we will buy a call that will grow in value but will need to be profitable in the short term, which is still realistic given the price history. We will buy STODM7 $14.50 June call. We shell out five cents ($0.05) per share. We decided to just buy five contracts, which cover 500 shares; we paid $25 (excluding fees).

Our profit target is 15 cents when the share price reaches $14.50. (Again, there is a tool available at the exchange website for "theoretical price value" or estimate of the value of option at a given price.) As the taker, we think the stock will move up strongly in two weeks; however, it will only be profitable above $14.55 (the strike price of $14.50 and the five-cent premium spent for the options contract).

Scaling in or Adding Positions

As the market is showing strong negative sentiment, we decided to add to our winning position that is riding the move down.

Buying Put B

We will add to our short position by buying more put options. We will keep to our position sizing and only use $140. At $14, we will buy a put that will grow in value; we take the next out of the money strike price. We will buy STOUW7 13.50 June put. We shell out 11.5 cents per share. With $140, we can get 12 contracts, which cover 1,200 shares.

Our profit target is 34.5 cents when the share price reaches $13.50. (There is a tool available at the exchange website for "theoretical price value" or estimate of the value of option at a given price). As the taker, we believe the stock will move down strongly in two weeks; however, it will only be profitable below $13.385 (the strike price of 13.50 and the 11.5-cent premium spent for the options contract).

Summary

The price continues its move down after a month; the share price is $13.14. We close all our options positions and hold on to our 500 shares. See Table 20 for a summary of our trading positions.

Strategy	Details	Number of Shares	Share Price				TOTAL
			14	14.76	14.00	13.14	13.14
			Value of Shares / Option				
Buy Stock		500	7000.00	7380.00	7000.00	6570.00	6570.00
Cov Call A	STOCM8 14.61 JUL	500		0.69	0.24	0.00	225.00
Buy Put A	STODK7 14 JUN	1400		0.095	0.315	0.89	1246.00
Cov Call B	STOCK8 13.67 JUL	500			0.655	0.31	172.50
Buy Call	STODM7 1450 JUN	500			0.05	0.015	0.015
Buy Put B	STOUW7 13.50 JUN	1200			0.115	0.45	540.00
							8766.66

Original Capital	7000.00
Profit / Loss	1766.66
Percent Gain (%)	25.24

Table 20 : Summary of Transactions

Profits

Covered call A—$225.00

Covered call B—$172.50

Buy put A—$1,246.00

Buy put B—$540.00

Loss

Share value—reduced to $6,570.00

Buy call—reduced to 0.015

Total of Profits and Losses

From our original capital of $7,000, the value of our stock holding and cash proceeds from all options trades is $1,766.64, a gain of 25.23% in one month, and we are still holding on to our shares.

By keeping to our position sizing rule and applying the principles of the velocity of money, we have increased our capital with low-risk trades that gave us high reward.

Notice that we have increased our capital in cash by 25%; in a year, we may be able to achieve 300% gain (25 × 12 months). Let's say we only achieve 100% gain, this will enable us to take out our original capital, thus further proceeds from our trading is coming from "nothing," letting us achieve returns of infinity.

Chapter 16: Conclusion

A Mom's Recipe to Start Trading

YOU WILL NEED:

1) Capital: $7,000

2) Full measure of self-mastery

3) A handful of knowledge

   a) Trading-specific: market, system,position sizing, trading concepts, and technical analysis, and all others in Must-haves list

   b) Financial: velocity of money, infinity

   c) Physical well-being

   d) Business planning

   e) Low-risk strategies

TIMING:

Trading should be done according to lifestyle. It is important to weave this around your lifestyle, ensuring that you take care of aspects in your life that give you purpose, joy, growth and overall wellbeing. This will help you to be "clear" when trading and also help to protect you from stress.

DIRECTIONS:

With the trading process, use a handful of knowledge and full measure of self-mastery.

1) Guided by the velocity of money that makes our investment grow, first, buy shares with your capital (e.g., $7,000).
   Rounded to the nearest hundred to make up options contracts
   (each contract is 100).

2) Then write a covered call on each contract. You can buy-
   write to ensure that there is no downside risk, or you can
   be patient and write-call when the price had moved up a
   notch for better profits in the end. Keep doing this with your
   shares. This will protect your shares and produce income to
   use for new opportunities.

3) When you've grown capital by at least 20% following our
   position-sizing rule, look for opportunity and seize it with a
   buy-call option or buy-put option, depending on your view
   of the market. This will grow more income.

Serve with a smile knowing that you will be investing
your money safely and trading it to increase returns despite
uncertainties.

What's the Catch?

My friend, Lorets Pacia, an IT professional in Singapore,
has been attending financial literacy / wealth building seminars
and told me one day, "I get a clearer view even macro econom-
ics which I'm really not interested in, why is it that I feel that
it seems so simple & easy to invest? Is there any catch or blind
spot that I need to learn?" Excellent questions don't you think?!
I didn't think of these when I started.   I guess being so excited
about the possibilities (and tired from slaving in my job back
then) I was in "shoot first, ask questions later mode". Anyway, my
answers to her and what I would like to share to you all is that :

1) You are moving to a stage in life that opens your mind to
   this - you are "stepping up", it's a natural consequence of
   your growth.

2) Marketing of the seminars and perhaps the content presented is made simple and easy (if it looks so hard who will go and do it?)

3) There are more and more opportunities to invest in "easily" because information is more accessible, and after that managing the investment can be done remotely -- the way technology has enabled our lives is a big factor to this.

The important thing is to continue learning about particular investments you want, then limit your risks- that's a good thing to learn and do before going in. You might think, OK, you've done your homework and jumped into the opportunity; in reality, you will only know for sure how an investment or trade would work when you're already in it. I mean, there will always be blind spots for anybody starting and even for experienced investor, a negative issue can always crop up (known or unknown). That's why it is important to limit your risk so you can fix as necessary. Or stay alive to do another deal. This is why position sizing is so important in trading. Having someone to hold your hand through the tough spots will also help greatly, benefit from their experience.

Another thing, as "fine print" of many financial products will tell you, "Results will vary and past success will not guarantee ongoing and increasing profitability." Think about the food you enjoy. (Is your mouth dripping yet?!) What do you think is the most important factor that made it so delicious? The recipe, the ingredients, or the cook? Someone can hand me an award-winning recipe but if the ingredients are incomplete or of poor quality, it could ruin the whole thing. And don't even think we can bake a cake without any sort of training or practice. Ting ting ting ting! Get it? Yes, YOU are responsible. Like any cook can tell you, that any recipe can be learnt, but having the skills to do things right would take time and practice. So, no matter how things may look easy, know that you need to go slow while developing your skills.

The good news is, you can trade profitably like only a woman can. Use wisdom gained from other areas of your life. Remember we can learn from our experiences in shopping, for shoes in particular, dressing up, mothering-aren't we lucky?! However, you have to apply your skills every single time. Nothing is guaranteed. A 7-year-old little girl named Abby Calimaran sums this up nicely with her guest post in my blog –"*you earn whatever you get!*"

May the Fierce be with you!

Low and slow in the Mekong River by AJ Mallari

Appendix: Should I Trade?

Table for Two: Real Estate and Trading

Most of my friends enthusiastic to trade always mention interest in real estate, so I thought I'd also share what I know about it side by side with trading. For a few years, even without cash to buy, we'd go inspecting houses for sale every weekend. When we spot a new development, we'd stop and check out their display. I would knock on walls to determine if materials satisfy soundproofing, look at color palettes, tiles (or carpet), fixtures, floor plans, and check out the surrounding area including transport options and shops. I'd also look at prices of comparable properties in the area and development plans/regulations by the local government. The "tipping point" comes after I've crunched the numbers and income; the equity value allows me to see if it's an "attractive risk." Is that a weird term? It's like stilettos with five-inch heels; it will cause some pain but it will surely make you look glamorous and you will still wear it.

A Reason for Every Season

There was a time when I was about to buy a one-bedroom apartment. There was already an exchange of contracts (i.e., two parties signed the contract). That meant I was buying the property and the developer/vendor was selling the property to me. I also put the clause "subject to finance," which means I only complete the purchase when my loan was approved— about a year from completion. Toward the end of the project, the marketing people who also arranged the loan said that the bank lowered its loan-to-value ratio (LVR) on the property. This means they were unwilling to lend as much as before; they were willing to lend 90% of the price then they changed it to 80%. So I needed to cough up a bigger downpayment (20%). This is when I sniffed the tightening in credit situation, so I got out. (Not easy. Want details? Email me!)

I focused on investing in "paper assets" like shares. Also around that time, my life situation was changing. I was going to have my first child and was planning to have the second shortly after. That would take time away from work for the next few years.

I think it is very important to bear in mind that having children is a big adjustment that you should consider in your financial strategy. You don't want to commit too much when there's the need to shoulder any big expense like a vacancy in a rental property or fees to maintain common property (e.g., the elevator). Try not to add financial worries to a delicate situation. When babies are growing up, it is a special time, enjoy it.

What I gather from my friends is that they think real estate is easier than trading, so they'd invest in real estate first. Hmm, I am not convinced that's the right approach to investing. Anyway, I thought the important consideration is to invest in something that will perform given the market conditions, and suitable to your overall life plan. Real estate is not as simple as it appears to be. Of course, trading is also not simple, but the key is being educated in both areas so you will know when they work best.

Also, I am telling you all these things I learned, but know that while great care is taken to present accurate and authoritative information, it is in no way tailored to any individual nor am I engaged in rendering legal, accounting, trading, or other professional services. If legal or other expert assistance is required, please seek competent professional advice.

18 Points to Consider When Investing:

Here's a list of considerations I recommend when investing:

1) Market Type

We've discussed that the prevailing market type will set the scene for your investment.

a) Real estate investments tend to perform well when the market goes up. In a sideways market, you need to add value like renovating or rezoning.

b) Trading allows you to execute strategies when the market goes up, down, and sideways.

Get a feel for when things are going great in investments, usually this would be a good economy. This is similar to situations when people are not worried about their jobs and they're more likely to spend on houses or take on more risks.

2) Fundamental Analysis

Is there value or growth in the investment, also note the risks it poses such as environment (for real estate) and management (for shares).

a) Real estate – rate it against criteria that make it a good investment and attract quality tenants. Things like accessibility to transport, work, and amenities as shopping centers and recreational facilities (e.g., beach, park, schools). It should also be structurally sound.

b) Trading -- determine whether the company is profitable or if it's achieving its profit forecasts. Does it have products in the pipeline or growth strategy? Is it a startup company with ''explosive'' products and services (e.g., Facebook with 500 million users is a startup with a lot of promise given its advertising edge to its users)? For shares, Warren Buffett has a business model for evaluating companies to invest; you can also check out William O'Neill's CANSLIM model.

3) Will it Require Financing and Leverage?

When you get a loan, the financial risks will always change; it can entail lowering the rates or increasing rates. You have to know that you can sufficiently service the loan; otherwise, you could lose your investment.

a) Real estate

Just think about the housing crisis in the U.S. at the start of the global financial crisis. Some people were committed to mortgages that started low but later jumped three times their original rate; that is just an insane amount of debt to shoulder. Many people were unable to service their loans and so they chose to foreclose. The loans that the bank will be willing to extend to you can also change during the course of your loan. Let's say during an economic recession, a commercial property can only be lent as much as 50% down from 60%. If you still want to invest in property without taking out a loan, look at the real estate investment trusts (REITs) or property syndication in your area.

b) Trading

In shares, the simplest way to invest is with your own money. You can just buy as many shares as you can afford. If you want, and if you have gotten a bit more sophisticated, then you can take out a loan (this is called "margin lending") using your shares as collateral. They will normally lend from 40% to 70%, depending on the quality of the company as assessed by your bank/broker.

In trading, if you're unable to pay your loan interest, the bank will liquidate your holdings and require you to pay additional cash if there's a shortfall in the sale of the shares. In real estate, they will get hold of your property, and if another property secures the equity on a second/ investment property, then the two properties will be in trouble. Understand your financing terms and conditions thoroughly.

4) **Income**

The purpose of investing is to get income while **we don't have to work**. This is called "passive income." You set it up and do its thing while you are busy with your life and, periodically, you get income from it. Sweet!

a) **Real Estate**

The allure of real estate is passive income, as long as your property has a tenant and pays rent, you get an income. Although you need to consider "net income" where your rental income is lessened by the expenses incurred by the property (e.g., loan payments, property maintenance, taxes), this can leave you with "negative cash flow" meaning you have to add cash to maintain the investment. (Why do it? An investor would weigh this loss against the value of the property and/or capital growth). Say, you're happy to shell out $50 a month because you bought the property with a small downpayment and the property is $100,000 below market value.

b) **Trading**

There are two kinds of incomes from Trading: passive income and trading income.

i) Passive income

(1) Dividend is usually from the "blue chips" or the well-established and profitable companies. They pay back their shareholders investment in the form of "dividends." They're regularly paid with a fixed or special dividend, a one-time payment for whatever reason the company deems fit.

(2) Interest earnings can come from shares/options and forex.

    (a) Shares/options. From an account maintenance point of view, when you have cash that you haven't committed to your trading that stays in a cash management account, you can get paid relatively high interest rates. My current bank, for example, pays 6.5% per year on cash. The earnings can pay some of your trading costs.

    (b) Forex. When trading currencies, you can earn an interest payment at a rate payable for the currencies, as you keep them in your trading account. I remember when the Aussie dollar was equivalent to 80 cents to $1 U.S. and started going up because our interest rate is much higher than the U.S. interest rate; it's now even past "parity" (meaning equal value). Imagine if you have been holding the Aussie dollar and earning the interest rate for, say, over one year, which went from 2.5% to 4.5%, your money would have grown from two incomes: the interest rate and the increase in value of the currency.

ii) Trading income

    From buying low and selling high as well as when you get more skilled and knowledgeable, you can also earn from selling high and buying low. Earning trading income requires a bit more activity than "passive income," but still, you need NOT spend 40 hours a week like a full-time job and get paid based on time.

This is an important consideration on your trading: you are able to trade markets and make money in both up and down directions. It does not only present more opportunities but it also manages your risk.

5) Costs: Opening and Closing

a) Real Estate

Profits are often squeezed by the high transaction costs to open and close real estate deal. The following is a typical transaction of buying an apartment "off the plan" in Australia (for investment purposes). For example, the property costs $277,000; then it was sold for $320,000 upon completion 12 months after, with $43,000 "profit"; however, there are costs to consider:

i) Legal fees—open/close = $2,500

ii) Real estate agent's fees include marketing (3.3%) = $10,560

iii) Government administration and search fee = $500

iv) Stamp duty = $8,900 (Australian government "tax" on purchase of property)

v) Deposit bond = $2,500 (paid instead of a 10% deposit, lessen the cash outlay)

Total acquisition costs = $24,960

Tax on gross profit at 30% = $5,412

Total transaction cost = $30,372

If selling after holding a property in a few years, there would be costs associated with getting the loan (administrative fees) or getting out of a fixed loan (exit fees or break fees), plus loan payments if the expenses is more than the income.

(You may refer to http://www.canstar.com.au/exit-fees/ for details.)

b) Trading

Trading by yourself through an online broker will generally save on your costs. Online share trading brokerage fees in Australia costs around $20; for options, it's around $45 per transaction, plus taxes. So to open and close, which involves two transactions, the cost is around $50 for shares and $100 for options. Samples of rates and fees may be accessed via this link: https://invest.etrade.com.au/RatesandFees/Default.aspx.

i)   With trading, some online brokers offer the active trader discounts on fees.

ii) Note that real estate costs *are much higher* than trading costs.

6) Continuing Expenses

a) Real Estate

These are the common periodic expenses for real estate investments:

i)   Monthly

(1) Loan payments

(2) Bank account fees

(3) Property management

(4) Transaction fees (debit/credit fees)

ii) Quarterly

(1) Property taxes

(2) Government services fees (e.g., garbage collection)

(3) Utility bills

iii) Annual

(1) Accountant fees (for yearly tax filing)

(2) Travel expenses (to inspect property could include airfare/hotel/taxi)

iv) Occasional (as the property gets older, more costs)

(1) Repairs

(2) Replacing fixtures and fittings (e.g., hot water system, plumbing)

a) **Trading**

These are the common monthly/quarterly costs for different types of traders:

i) Private traders

(1) Internet subscription

(2) Phone service

(3) Continuing education costs for seminar, books, materials, and others

ii) Long-term investor

Same or less expenses as above. No extra expense to buy and hold shares or ETFs, as there is no time restriction to hold these investments

iii) Short-term/day trader

Since there is more trading activity, chances are, the trading style would need more real-time data and sophisticated tools. Here are some examples:

(1) Software

(2) Subscription to more sophisticated trading platform

(3) Subscription to market data

iv) Professional traders belonging to large funds or those who operate funds can also incur costs relating to being members of an exchange and other costs to comply with regulation.

Be aware of the high costs of how you invest or maintain the investment. Oh, I know some people would say, "it's okay" or that "it's tax deductible." Yeah, right, but you have to cough up the money in the first place. From a cash flow perspective, that is not good.

7) Growth Factors

What conditions will allow increase in value of your investment?

a) Real Estate

The growth of real estate is generally related to a few factors:

i) Good news. Good economy, job growth, increased migration, or changing demographics can increase demand that pushes prices up.

ii) Scarcity. The limited land areas along waterways that feature relaxing views and create exclusivity attract premium and increase its value, as people compete for these kinds of properties.

iii) Inflation. With people's expenses going up, people also invest in real estate so they can benefit from increased value of their assets; it's like a protection from inflation.

d) Trading

i) Good news

(1) Good economy with job growth tends to favor shares in general; companies tend to do well in environment with high demand and consumer spending.

(2) Demand growth – allow growth in revenues resulting to more value appreciation for shares and commodities of basic needs like food, metal, oil, and other consumer goods (phones or computers) as well as cars.

(3) When people have more buying power, prices tend to go up (called inflation) and governments raise interest rates to try to slow them down. Higher interest rates benefit the currency of that country where the current conditions of steady rise is seen (e.g., Indonesian rupiah, Australian dollar, and South Korean won).

ii) Bad News

(1) War tends to increase the appeal of gold as safe haven and oil as a precious energy source that wars tend to consume.

(2) Recession or slow economic growth is the time when interest rates are lowered by central banks to make more money available to people (with loans). When interest rates are cut by 0.50%, for example, a person with $250,000 loan will pay about $100 *less* on interest repayments a month and can buy other goods/services; thus, stock prices could go up despite the economic recession.

(3) Low U.S. dollar. Because this is the world's reserve currency used to price many commodities in demand around the world, the movements of U.S. dollar affect the price of gold, oil, and other agricultural products. An asset may moves in the opposite direction (have an inverse relationship) with the other commodities, i.e., if the U.S. dollar downtrends (weakens), the price of commodities go up because the dollar becomes more "affordable" to nondollar holders.

Notice that, in trading, there are always opportunities on both the up and down market, and at time, even the sideways market! There are financial instruments that could be traded to perform according to different market conditions.Anything can happen in the world, really. In addition, a girl has to be prepared, don't you think?! That is why a pair of shoes with a classic design is a must-have wardrobe staple! It doesn't matter if it's summer or winter, you'd always be in the thick of the action! Trading is the same as it is an all-weather business! Now, you know that like smart shopping, this is a must-have skill!

8) Create Value

Can you increase the value of your investment by making it more useful or beautiful?

a) Real Estate

If it is an apartment or unit, then you are limited to improving the interior of your property.

i) Renovate or capitalize on key areas like the kitchen or bathroom.

ii) Add more space, enclose a balcony so it has indoor use, or add storage.

iii) Make it attractive; all the apartment owners can vote to do a facelift for the whole building (e.g., rendering or repainting, change of windows).

If it's a house or structure on its own title, in addition to the above.

iv) Enclose a carport to make it a garage (more secure with more storage possibilities).

v) Add an attic or a clever use of existing spaces such as storage or children's nook.

vi) Add environmentally friendly features such as solar heater, sunroof, or plant life.

vii) Add a "granny flat" or separate self-contained studio you can rent out.

viii) Rezone --some residential property can be rezoned for commercial or mixed use. Let's say the area is getting heavy on traffic, a house may be converted to a display center, a doctor's clinic, a café, or an art gallery that benefits from people or vehicles going past.

b) Trading

With your own powers, you generally can't do anything to improve the value of an investment. You can't raise the value of your bank shares by taking out a larger loan. Although, collectively, the banks could be more profitable as many people take out more loans and pay on its terms. To create value in trading, what you need to do is to improve your skills and knowledge. Remember I said earlier that the key to generate income consistently in trading is self-mastery: the doing when something needs done and NOT doing when it is not supposed to be done (self-control). So keep learning about yourself, address your weaknesses, and cultivate positivity.

9) Expansion Strategy

Astute business and investing always consider how to expand business and income potential.

a) Real Estate

i) Redevelop. You can redevelop a property. Let's say build a dual-occupancy unit or duplex where two families can have separate living spaces, provided the land area is big enough to satisfy the local government guidelines. In one area we were looking at, the minimum is 600 m² and the frontage (how wide it is at the front) must be 20 m². Some areas designate 1,000 m² to be the minimum, with 500 m² needed and given its own land title. These rules could change in the future.

ii) Some investors take a long-term view and buy land that is close to the city (an hour commute or so) to sell or develop later. Note that this could be 10 to 20 years and is largely uncertain; you still have to work with the local government for approval. Check development plans. An airport or rail line could massively increase the value of your landholding.

b) Trading

i) You can expand your trading business by branching out to other markets. Many companies operate in many major economies and are listed in more than one exchange (or country). For example, since you already know the company and able to trade it profitably, you can choose to trade it in other exchanges like BHP, the biggest mining company in the world that has headquarters in Australia. It is traded in Australian Stock Exchange, London Stock Exchange, New York Stock Exchange, and Johannesburg Stock Exchange. You can also easily do this on forex, oil, and gold, i.e., trading it on different time zones, e.g., the Japanese yen, which is a very popular currency for trading. You may choose to start your trading day in the Asian time zone and then follow the sun to the European time zone and then to the U.S. time zone. (Sleep optional!)

ii) You can also trade other investments or instruments related to the one you are currently trading. You can do this when you are trading something and know that other investments move with opposite effect (an inverse relationship). For example, when the Japanese yen is stronger, stock prices of some Japanese companies like Toyota and Canon also go down because they generate most of their sales outside of Japan and are paid in U.S. dollars in their terms of trade. With a stronger yen, there will be less money (yen) for every dollar for these companies.

iii) System. You can develop a new system and take advantage of more opportunities. For example, a system that achieves 5% per month writing call options in a sideways market but does not perform as well during bull market. To take advantage of the opportunity of an uptrending market, develop a system that will not cap profits and be able to ride the trend.

iv) Automation. By automating your system, you can certainly handle more funds to manage. For example, you can go from five hundred thousand to five million easily. It also makes the position sizing more accurate, but allocate with discipline. It takes away the human factor, with less error, and will trade without emotion, just following the rules you have set with your system. Also with increased efficiency, you can focus on growing your trading business by trading other markets or by accepting new funds.

10) **Liquidity**

Liquidity is one of the most talked-about qualities of an investment. It is important because it gives flexibility to the investor as well as safety in that when times are difficult, you can get out of your investment and keep losses small.

a) **Real Estate**

Any homeowner knows this: you cannot sell a house in a day or two. Even if you are able to find a buyer willing to cough up the money you are asking for at the first day you sell, there are many laws that control the completion of the deal. Consider the following:

i) Cooling-off period. When the buyer gives a written offer to buy, there is still a minimum period, let's say 24 hours, that they can back out.

ii) Inspection period. Laws try to give people a fair chance to make sure goods and properties are in a condition that is acceptable to the buyer. At this time, a building inspector or "valuer" may be brought in to check the soundness of the structure, security, and any pest issues the property's worth compared with the market. This can take one to five days, depending on the availability of the professionals.

iii) Settlement period. Normally, a property is bought with a bank loan, and you would have to deal with the government's administrative procedures about the change of ownership. Some sellers use this time as well to look for alternative accommodation. This period can take around six weeks of negotiation between the two parties.

If the seller is in a hurry to settle, this is a chance to get a better price.

b) **Trading**

There is varying degree of liquidity in the financial markets. Remember, this is the ease of getting in or out of the investment. Companies with a big amount of shares available to the public and long history of profitability are called "blue chips," also considered as the more liquid shares. Smaller companies with smaller number of shares may be harder to get out of at times. In the forex market, an estimated $3.98 trillion dollars change hands a day. It is very very liquid; thus, it attracts many traders. As for time, trading transactions to close can take two to four days.

11) **Access to Funds or Investment**

This is similar to liquidity; however, let's talk about getting some money out or getting back in the investment.

a) **Real Estate.** You don't have to sell your property to get some money out, and this is one attraction of real estate. You can instead gain access to funds and equity with your home loan.

i)   Structure your loan to have a redraw facility. Banks may have a loan product where you can redraw your equity. Normally, it would be set up such that you can put in extra payments to the loan (lowering your debt) and get funds as needed.

ii) Refinance. If you have not structured your loan for a redraw facility or if your property has appreciated and you want to get back some equity, you can refinance. This means you are getting a new loan and paying back the old loan. For example, the original loan is $100,000, which is 80% of the value of the property worth $125,000, then the property increased in value to $170,000. You can refinance with 80% loan-to-value ratio and your new loan is $136,000. You then pay your old loan of $100,000, which makes $36,000 available to you.

b) Trading

i)   You will have to sell your investments to be able to gain access to funds. Although, unlike real estate, you can sell just a *part* of it.

ii) Financial markets are volatile, so in case you have sold your shares at a high price and profit, you can always jump back in when it goes down.

iii) You can also take advantage of derivatives like call options to roll up your investment without fully committing your cash.

12) Calculating Payoff

In calculating payoff, you are mapping the point you get breakeven, profit, or loss. Having this roadmap will definitely allow you to rethink whether to take that direction, employ any tricks if you can to get the desired result, or even save resources.

a) **Real Estate**

   i) Pay off loan and debt repayments. Do you know that when you pay your loan more frequently (every fortnight instead of monthly), you pay LESS interest on your home loan? I used a home loan repayment calculator for a loan of $300,000 with a 7.25% interest rate and loan term of 30 years:

   If you're paying monthly, you pay $2,046.53 with a total interest payable of $436,750 for the life of the loan.

   If you're paying fortnightly, you pay $1,022.83 with a total interest payable of $325,546 for the life of the loan.

   That's $111,204 that you save and don't have to pay at all *just because you invested five minutes* in checking your loan repayments payoff. You found that reducing your principal more frequently would save you a ton of money.

   ii) Flipping a property, I had a friend asking me to join in buying a worn-out property, renovating it, and selling it quickly for a profit. I did a quick study of the figures that looked something like this:

   (1) Calculate all expenses in opening and closing the transaction, including real estate agent's fees, stamp duty, taxes, lawyer's fees, bank fees, and so forth.

   (2) Calculate the renovation expenses (cost of a new carpet, paint, kitchen, bathroom, other fixtures, etc.). If you want to attract high bids, you have to present the property beautifully.

(3) Calculate and allocate the loan repayments from buying and selling the property; this could take three to six months.

(4) Calculate the total expenses; add 10% to 15% for slippage (going over budget).

(5) Assess market value of similar properties; you need to be in an attractive and competitive price point if you plan to sell and flip quickly.

Let's say the property is $400,000, and the total expenses for the project are $60,000, then the property should sell for not less than $460,000 (your breakeven point). Now, if the market value of similar properties in the area is $460,000 to $480,000, then you will either only breakeven or get a $20,000 profit. Considering the whole risk of the project, it doesn't seem to be worth it.

I came back to him with the conclusion that we need to buy the property in a popular suburb with a steep discount—around 20% to 30% *below* market value and sell quickly—taking long will eat up profits.

Knowing the payoff of the transaction before starting, you'd be better informed whether to do the project or how to go about doing it.

b) Trading

With shares or options, it's easy to plot payoff and breakeven points.

i) Say, with a stock that costs $5 each, you buy 500, and the total investment is equal to $2,500.

ii) Then add the costs of opening and closing the transaction, which is just the broker fees, and the government charges, which may be around $50.

iii) Take the total investment of $2,500 and the total cost of $50 to arrive at $2,550. Then divide this by the number of shares (1,000); your breakeven point for each stock is $5.10. For any price that moves above $5.10, you're profitable. For any price that moves below $5.10, you have a loss.

Starting out though, I hear about people wanting to "diversify," thus they think they're doing a "good job" by only risking a small amount on any one-company stock. (I did this too!) However, the stock price has to make a BIG move in order to be profitable. The shareholding would be languishing at a "loss" for a long time before they are profitable. Instead of "diversifying" stock holding, they'd have better opportunity to profit with being "focused" on one stock and managing the trade carefully instead. For example, with a $50 transaction cost, a 500-share holding only needs to gain 2% to breakeven, while a 100-share holding needs to gain 10% to breakeven. Mapping out payoff, is helpful in determining the number of shares to buy and the opportunities you can have. (For instance, how many times can your share rise 10% in one year?). Check the detailed Comparison of Gains table that I posted in my blog www.highheeledtraders.com Book Resources page.

13) Depreciation

"Decline in value" is the general definition of depreciation.

a) Real Estate

As time passes, steel materials rust, masonry can crumble, and chemicals for adhesive and paint lose strength. It is then reasonable to expect that buildings made up of these materials will slowly decay. Therefore, the value of a building goes down. So in real estate, brand-new properties are popular with investors. With a new property, every year, you can claim depreciation as a tax-deductible expense of the building and chattels (or fixtures like the plumbing, doors). As an example, for a building and structure worth $290,000, you can claim depreciation of building and chattels around $7,200. This will have the effect of lessening the personal income tax you have to pay if a property is in your name.

A seminar I attended even trumpeted this as a good thing because you are lowering the taxes you pay or get a big tax refund. But don't get too excited because when you sell the property, the depreciated amount will be considered in the tax calculations. I know some people who got a shock from a tax bill in one financial year because they had a property sold that year but claimed depreciation in the previous years. A discussion on this topic, however, is beyond the scope of this book. Do check with a tax professional before doing anything.

b) Trading

In trading financial markets, you will hear "currency depreciation" which refers to the loss of value of a country's currency against one or more currencies.

Depreciation, as explained in real estate discussion, does not apply in trading.

14) Taxation

First, let me say that it is important to study tax guidelines. Tax agencies provide the public excellent information and armed with this knowledge; do consult with your accountant for tax matters. For one, there are different tax rates for different structures, people!

a) **Real Estate.**

The following are common taxes that apply to investing in real estate investments:

i) Land tax. Based on the value of your property, land tax is an annual payment to the local government. I tried to look up the justification and purpose of this tax but I didn't find any! The following link would give you more information: http://www.osr.nsw.gov.au/taxes/land/general/

ii) Stamp duty. This is a payment to the government when you buy property in Australia—what luck! Other countries like New Zealand, Singapore, and the United States do not have this tax. There are exemptions, like when you are a first home buyer, and up to a certain threshold. It is applicable to most investment property.

iii) Capital gains tax (CGT). When you sell or give away an asset that exceeds its original value, you may be required to pay this tax.

iv) Income tax. This is an annual tax on your income for the year; this includes rent income received from your real estate investments, dividend income, and interest earnings.

v) Estate tax or inheritance tax. Isn't there a "joke" that says the only permanent things in the world are death and taxes? A special tax combines both! Estate tax is tax payable on the transfer of assets of a deceased person.

vi) Goods and services tax (GST)/value-added tax. The property itself may be exempt, but services relating to real estate like property management and any other goods you buy to maintain property (e.g., curtains, dishwasher) is subject to GST.

b) Trading

There are fewer taxes to pay in trading:

i) Capital gains tax (CGT). When you sell or give away an asset for more than the original value, you may be liable to pay this tax. Say you bought shares at $12 and sold at $20, you have to pay tax on the $8 (less fees).

ii) Income tax. This is an annual tax on your income for the year. It includes dividend income and interest earnings (from your holding account for trading).

Now just a word about dividends, if they are "fully franked," i.e., tax has already been paid by the company on the profits from which dividends are paid, then individuals may not need to pay tax on it. Australia, New Zealand, and the United Kingdom have similar system called "dividend imputation." Tax laws vary from country to country and business structure so check with your accountant.

iii) Goods and services tax/value-added tax. Shares may be exempt, but related services like brokerage and clearing are subject to GST.

15) Legally All Yours

It is best of course to consult with lawyers/solicitors regarding legal issues. I thought I'd just give you a few memorable (and some painful) lessons on legal matters from my past life.

a) **Real Estate**

  i) Ownership rules. Pay attention to this. You don't want to be on the hunt for property you cannot own. In Australia, there are constraints to what nonpermanent residents and citizens can own; only new properties are available for investment.

  ii) Contract for sale. It is wise to check the whole sheaf of papers enclosed in a contract for sale. Let's pay attention to the following:

    (1) The property has registered liens, which can be a complexity. A "lien" is like a legal claim to the property, which can prevent it from being sold or slow down the process.

    (2) If the property is yet to be built or is off the plan, it should have an attachment of all fixtures and fittings to *exact* specifications. For example, check the dishwasher brand and capacity. This is an area where the builder developer could go cheap if they are vague in the contract and could be very disappointing when you see everything completed.

    (3) If you have plans to rebuild or redevelop, note the layout of the land, where the easements are located. Easements can be used for the transport of services like water, gas, telephone, and the like. In addition, because maintenance or repair is required on such services, you cannot build on the surface, thus you need to consider this if you have plans to develop the property further.

      (a) Exchange of contracts. This seals the deal between buyer and seller for the purchase of property. A deposit is payable at this point, usually 10% of the sale price. If the buyer does not want to proceed with the sale at any time after that, goodbye deposit! It is forfeited in favor of the seller. Check if there is a cooling-off period (e.g., five days from exchange).

(b) Sunset clause. This is applicable to properties sold "off the plan" or those that are still being constructed. In Australia, development projects are required to have a "final completion date." After which, your obligation to the contract evaporates. (You know, like the sunset, there is no more light after the sun goes down.)

(c) Settlement time limits. After the exchange of contracts, you proceed to the settlement to complete the transaction. This is when the transfer of title is done and the balance of the purchase price is paid (deposit is paid at exchange of contracts) and you become the legal owner of the property.

(d) Rental guarantees. Some sellers will entice buyers with rental guarantees. This means the buyers are willing to pay rent for the property after settlement. They could offer two weeks or so. We took the bait on this one, as it seems straightforward, BUT when we actually got a tenant to occupy in a week, instead of paying rent for the agreed two weeks, they just want to pay the number of days it is actually vacant. Now, that's frustrating because we offered $200 discount on the rent so they could move in quickly, as it was nearing the Christmas holiday period.

This link from the Department of Fair Trading in New South Wales could be handy for your information gathering: http://www. fairtrading.nsw.gov.au/Tenants_and_home_ owners/Buying_property.html

b) Trading

I have nothing much to write here. (What a relief!) Trading has few legal complexities. Only ownership rules come to mind; your financial institution or broker can have account opening guidelines you can use. Usually, they comply with local ownership rules for foreign investors, tax, terrorism, or anti-money laundering laws.

16) Systems

I am often awed living in these times. You want to send a letter, no need for pen and paper, stamp, or walking to the post office. You just send an email, which is faster and cheaper too. You can say a system is a series of steps that achieves something. In investing and trading, you need systems to work for you.

a) **Real Estate.** A very good thing about investing on real estate is that once you have a new property and a property manager, there's nothing much to do. It really is a passive investment. The property itself is composed of many systems: electric system, plumbing system, and ventilation, among others. The property manager you would choose should have business systems that easily and promptly pay you and inform you of the income, expenses, and anything that requires your action.

b) Trading

One of my BIG lessons in trading, which I hope you also remember, is to "trade a system that fits you" (from the book *Market Wizards* by Jack Schwager and echoed in Dr. Van Tharp's book, *Trade Your Way to Financial Freedom*).

There are three ways to get a trading system:

i) **Create your own system.** You can create your own system (your rules for entry, profit-taking, stop, etc.), then you can practice trade, test, and revise as needed until it is profitable. At the start, you may have to follow your system manually (making sure you exercise self-control), have it automated (hire an IT professional), and then it will give you passive income. If you follow your rules—even if it's not computerized—you can achieve income of stellar returns; say targeting only 3% per month × 12 months, that's 36% per year. (Compare with 7% bank interest!) One of my systems produced extra income for me even with a seesawing market. It afforded me to visit my parents overseas, celebrate the new baby, and the capital was still working for me after coming back from vacation. How good is that?!

ii) **Professional system.** The people who trade professionally (fund managers, hedge funds, mutual funds, etc.) have computerized trading systems with which to put their millions of dollars to work for their clients. They can achieve upward of 20% with their systems. You can invest this way, but be sure to "trade a system that fits you." If the fund manager's system needs you to tolerate a loss of 50%, can you take it?

iii) **Buy a system.** Mind you, systems for sale cost thousands of dollars. If you want to buy a system, be sure it is as close to your trading beliefs and rules as much as possible.

17) **Location and Environmental Factors**

a) **Real Estate**

They say the three most important things in real estate is location, location, location.

Investment properties in a good location command increasing prices and rents. They should be close to public transport system, places of work, and amenities such as shopping, schools, and recreational areas (e.g., parks, beach, sports centers).

However, there are environmental factors that should be considered in buying or building an investment property. A variety of environmental forces affecting life and property (earthquakes, floods, tsunami, volcanic eruption, blizzards, hurricanes, forest fires) can be painful financially.

You might be able to check this with locals or government development plans that may carry historical information of damages from environmental factors. In the recent widespread flooding in Queensland, they say the same thing happened 30 years ago, and so this has been a clue for flatlands or low-lying areas close to river systems. Just be careful and know the environmental risks to your investment, ensure that the structures comply with building codes and get the appropriate protection.

b) **Trading**

i) Access. With the mighty Internet and telecommunications services, we can do so much more in less time and even while on the move in remote areas. I got online in an Asian island where I checked my trading account in Australia! Broadband rocks! In trading, you can access your online broker to place trades or monitor them wherever you are or whatever time you choose—giving you flexibility, even freedom!

ii) Opportunity. Another good thing about trading is that you are not restricted to do business by your location; you can take advantage of opportunities outside of your home country. Consider, for instance, being able to trade shares in the New York Stock Exchange even through your local broker or with a financial institution of your target country. You can participate in the growing economic prosperity of other countries by trading ETFs for that country (e.g., Indonesia, Brazil) and by trading their appreciating currencies.

18) Protection

The recent earthquake and tsunami that hit Japan did not only destroy lives and properties in Japan, these calamities made a disastrous effect on real estate and trading in financial markets as well. The Japanese yen strengthened, and this had the effect of driving down the value of Japanese exporters. With risks rising due to the nuclear crisis, companies mining uranium and other nuclear fuels (many in Australia) dived. There was also a widespread selling in other markets, including the normal safe haven of gold being converted to cash. You wonder, "Is there any way to get some protection when these things happen?"

a) **Real Estate.**

i) Insurance is a common tool to protect property:

(1) Home insurance. It insures the building structure, often required by banks.

(2) Home contents insurance. It insures the personal property of occupiers.

(3) Landlord insurance. It insures one from loss of rental income and/or damage caused by tenants and others.

ii) Where the insurance companies do not cover damage from environmental factors or what they call the "acts of God" ("force majeure"), there might be available coverage from the government. An example of this is the Earthquake Commission (EQC) established by the government of New Zealand. It covers residential property owners for "damage caused by earthquake, natural landslip, volcanic eruption, hydrothermal activity, tsunami, including storm, flood, or fire" caused by environmental forces. Check out their website: http://www.eqc.govt.nz/.

b) Trading

You might ask, "Can I be insured against a fall in my shares as I am going to retire soon?" In fact, you can! You just have to know about options, briefly discussed in "Learn to Last Financially" and "Keep Your Options Open Often."

For example, to protect the value of your assets, you can buy put options paying 30 cents, but you now have the right to sell your stock at $20. Even if the stock price falls to $18 you have the right to sell at $20. You have protected the value of your stock. (Thank heavens!)

Options are widely available and you can check with your local exchange whether they are available for you to trade. In the United States, you'd find one of the oldest, largest, and most diverse marketplace for options and other derivatives at the Chicago Mercantile Exchange, where they have options on forex, whole stock market index, ETFs, and they even have options traded to protect profits from "washing away" due to rainfall. I like that!

Visit http://www.cmegroup.com/ for details.

Glossary

arbitrage
The taking advantage of "windows of opportunity" or loophole in a system to make money with low risk.

asset allocation
A way of deciding how to assign amounts of money from total funds available.

average true range
The average over a number of days of the true range.

band trading
A style of trading applied to financial instruments that are deemed to move in a range of price.

bearish
Having an outlook that the market will go down in the future.

bid-ask spread

blue-chip
Highly profitable publicly-traded companies.

bonds
Bonds are debt instruments that represent an obligation on the part of the issuer to repay the debt.

breakout
A move up from a range, sideways movement or consolidation.

bullish
Having an outlook that the market will go up in the future.

call option   A call option is a contract that allows
                          you to buy at a price you want at a
                          future date. It is a right to buy, not an
                          obligation.

candlestick   A type of bar chart, developed by the
                          Japanese, in which the price range be-
                          tween the open and close is either a
                          white rectangle (if the close is higher)
                          or black rectangle (if the close is lower).

capital   The funds an investor/trader have to
                          take opportunities.

capitalization   The amount of money in the underlying
                          stock of a company.

commodities   Physical products that are traded at a
                          futures exchange. Examples of such
                          products are metals, energy, agricultur-
                          al produce.

consolidation   A period of low volatility, prices move
                          in a limited range and does not seem to
                          trend.

contract   A single unit of a commodity, option
                          or financial instrument. For example, a
                          single unit or contract of option is 100
                          shares, a single unit of oil is one barrel.

discretionary trading A way of doing trading that depends
                          on a trader's instincts as opposed to a
                          systematic approach or have system
                          then use discretion in exits and position
                          sizing.

diversification   Investing in markets that are not related to each other to reduce risk of financial ruin

drawdown   Loss of value of your account due to unprofitable trades or "paper losses"

entry   One of the rules comprising your system that you follow to get into a trading position

equities   Shares secured by ownership of the company

equity   The money in your account

exit   One of the rules comprising your system that you follow to get out of a trading position

financial freedom   Financial status of having income that you don't have to work for that is greater than expenses

forex   The foreign exchange. A global market in foreign currencies made by large banks worldwide. Today there are also much smaller companies that allow you to trade forex, but they take the side of the bid-ask spread opposite from you.

fundamental analysis   A way of analyzing the market to determine its supply-and-demand characteristics. In equities markets, fundamental analysis determines the value, the financial, management and many other data of a particular stock.

futures   This is a market that deals on contracts of specific assets at a specific price and time.

gap   A part of a price chart that may show a lack of trades. This occurs after the close of the market on one day and the open of the market on the next day

indicator   Market data presented in a supposedly meaningful way to help traders and investors in making trading decisions.

instruments

intermarket analysis   The use of the price moves in one market that may move another market. For example, the price of gold might change depending on what will happen with the US dollar.

investing   Refers to a buy and hold strategy. If you are in and out frequently or you are willing to both go long and short, then that will be considered a trading activity.

leverage   A term used to describe a control of large investment using a small amount of capital.

limit order   An order placed with your broker in which you specify a limit as to how much you want to buy or sell. If your broker cannot get this price or better, the order is not executed.

liquidity   The ease of getting in and out of the market easily.

long

A position entered when expecting a rise in price / value.

market maker

A trader, usually associated with a broker, bank or investment firm that makes a two-way price to either buy or sell a security, currency or contract.

market order

An order to buy or sell at the current market price. Market orders are executed quickly upon confirmation of the trader.

mechanical trading

A form of trading that uses computer program to execute trades, with no further human decision-making.

moving average

A method of presenting averages in price usually on a nominated number of days. For example, 20-day moving average, 30-day moving average. The average is computed from the most recent day, hence, with every new day, the previous last day is dropped.

option

An option is a contract between two parties giving the taker (buyer) the right, but not the obligation, either to Buy or Sell a parcel of shares at a specified price on or before a specified date."

options spread

A trading strategy by which one opens two positions at the same time and profits from the difference in the price of the two positions.

passive income

An income received independent of your time and effort. Money is working for you.

percent-risk model

A position sizing model based on a certain percentage of equity

position sizing

Position sizing identifies "how much" you're risking for each trade

prediction

A guess about what will happen in the future.

price/earnings ratio

A ratio of the shareprice to its earnings. For example, if a $10 share earns $1 per year, it has a price/earnings ratio of 10.

put option

A put option is a contract that allows you to sell at a price you want at a future date. It is a right to sell, not an obligation.

R multiple

A term used to express trading results in terms of the initial risk (1R)

R value

A term used to express the initial risk (1R) taken in a given position.

random

An event that happens by chance or cannot be predicted.

resistance

Price level at the top part of a range that seems to form a lid on the price movement.

retracement

A price movement in the opposite of the previous trend.

risk
A possibility that can occur given an action or inaction that will result to a loss.

seasonal trading
Trading based on seasonal patterns due to climate or demand cycles.

shares
Also called shares. Each share represents ownership of a company's assets less its debt (net assets).

short
A position entered when expecting a fall in price / value.

sideways market
A market that does not move up on a clear trend up or down.

slippage
The difference in the price you expect to pay and what you actually pay for.

speculating
Taking a trading position in expected price direction.

spreading
As used in options, the simultaneous buying and selling of contracts to profit from the price difference of the two positions.

stalking
A term used in looking for an opportunity to get into a trading position.

stop
An allowance you are giving your trade to move in your favor. If the stop is breached, you get out of the trade to limit your losses.

stochastic
An indicator for overbought or oversold conditions.

support

Price level at the bottom part of a range. A shareprice usually has difficulty falling below this level.

swing trading

A term that refers to a short-term trading that aims to capture quick moves in the market.

system

A set of rules for trading that typically have entry, stop, profit-taking exit and position sizing.

trading

Opening a position in the market, either long or short, with the expectation of either closing it at a huge profit.

trailing stop

A stop that is adjusted as the trade moves along with the market.

trend following

A concept used in trading that seek to profit from following prevailing trends.

trendline

A line connecting prices that will show a trend up or down.

value trading

A concept in which trading positions are opened in the market because they represent good value-they are usually based on the net assets of the company.

volatility

The up or down movement of a price in a given time period.

References

Books

Jeffrie, Sally. "The Girls' Book of Glamour". London, Buster Books, 2008

Jenkins, Alexander. *Follow the Model.* New York : Gallery Books, 2009

Schwager, Jack. *Market Wizards.* New York: New York Institute of Finance, 1988

_____. *The New Market Wizards.* New York: HarperCollins, 1992

Tate, Christopher. *Understanding Options Trading in Australia.* Melbourne : Wrightbooks, 1997

Tharp, Van. *Super Trader.* Lake Lucerne, 2011.

Tharp, Van. *The Definitive Guide to Expectancy and Position Sizing.* Cary, NC: Van Tharp Institute, 1998-1994.

Tharp, Van. *The Peak Performance Course for Traders and Investors.* Cary, NC: Van Tharp Institute, 1998-1994.

Tharp, Van, D.R. Barton, and Steve Sjuggerud. *Safe Strategies for Financial Freedom.* Cary, NC: Van Tharp Institute, 1998-1994.

Tharp, Van, and Brian June. *Financial Freedom Through Electronic Day Trading.* Cary, NC: Van Tharp Institute, 1998-1994.

Periodicals (Webpages)

Burton, Katherine and Roben Farzad. "Soros Goes Private as Golden Era of Rock Star Traders Concludes." Bloomberg, 29 July 2011. < http://www.bloomberg.com/news/2011-07-28/soros-goes-private-as-golden-era-of-rock-star-traders-ends-with-dodd-frank.html >

Crippen, Alex. "Warren Buffett: NBA Star LeBron James "Has His Head Screwed On Right". CNBC.com, 2 Jan 2009. <http://www.cnbc.com/id/28469512/Warren_Buffett_NBA_Star_LeBron_James_Has_His_Head_Screwed_On_Right

Dutra, Ana. "Motherhood and Leadership Agility." *Forbes.com*, 9 May 2011 <http://www.forbes.com/sites/anadutra/2011/05/09/motherhood-and-leadership-agility/>

Kearns, Jeff and Nina Mehta. "Options Trading Heads for Record Volume as U.S. Institutions Increase Use." *Bloomberg.com* 12 July 2011. <http://www.bloomberg.com/news/2011-07-12/options-trading-heads-for-record-volume-as-u-s-institutions-increase-use.html >

Lambert, Emily. "More Women are Trading-Here's Why." *Forbes.com*, 4 April 2011. < http://www.forbes.com/sites/emilylambert/2011/04/04/more-women-are-trading-heres-why/

Liberto, Jenny. "Personal Finance Advice from Barack Obama". *CNN Money*, 9 June 2011. <http://money.cnn.com/2011/06/09/news/economy/obama_financial_advice/index.htm >

O'Malley, Zack. "Why Diddy will be Hip Hop's First Billionaire." Forbes.com, 16 March 2011 http://blogs.forbes.com/zackomalleygreenburg/2011/03/16/why-diddy-will-be-hip-hops-first-billionaire/

Tamar, Lewin. "A Hemline Index, Updated." New York Times, 18 Oct 2008. http://www.nytimes.com/2008/10/19/weekinreview/19lewin.html

Wang, Shirley. "China Entices Scientists to Return Home." Wall Street Journal, 18 Nov 2010. <http://online.wsj.com/article/SB10001424052748704648604575619950288337066.html

http://s.wsj.net/public/resources/documents/st_madoff_victims_20081215.html

---

eBooks

Eker, T. Harv. *Secrets of the Millionaire Mind*. Harper Business.

Websites

Australian Tax Office http://www.ato.gov.au/

Australian Stock Exchange (ASX): http://www.asx.com.au/resources/shares-education.htm

Bloomberg http://www.bloomberg.com/

Chicago Board of Options http://www.cboe.com/data/volatility-indexes/volatilityindexes.aspx

Chicago Mercantile Exchange http://www.cmegroup.com/

CNN http://www.cnn.com/

Department of Fair Trading New South Wales http://www.fairtrading.nsw.gov.au

http://www.educationtaxrefund.gov.au/what-can-i-claim.html

http://www.elle.com/Fashion/Trend-Reports/Top-10-The-Spring-2011-Trend-Report

Earthquake Commission http://www.eqc.govt.nz/.

Forbes Magazine http://www.forbes.com/

Investment University. http://www.investmentu.com/

Ken Long's blog http://kansasreflections.wordpress.com/

New York Stock Exchange (NYSE) Publications: http://www.nyse.com/

http://www.nyse.com/about/education/1098034584990.html

http://www.nyse.com/about/education/1022630233386.html

Reuters http://www.reuters.com/

St. Louis Federal Reserve http://research.stlouisfed.org/fred2/categories/32242

Singapore Exchange (SGX): http://www.sgx.com/wps/portal/marketplace/mp-en/investor_centre

The Huffington Post http://www.huffingtonpost.com/

The Wall Street Journal http://asia.wsj.com, http://online.wsj.com

YouTube http://www.youtube.com/watch?v=QnG5yAloXAA

About the Author

Charmel Delos Santos is a private trader, mother of three, systems analyst and ex-beauty queen wannabe.

Women and Community Charmel grew up in the Philippines with strong feminine presence in her family life. At a young age, she worked with village women in the family business. She studied in exclusive schools for girls, served the community and church as a choir member, and later became Ambassador of Goodwill to the Ship for Southeast Asian Youth Program (SSEAYP). She presently volunteers in a mother's group/playgroup and a member of United Nations Women National Committee Australia.

Fashion and Beauty Charmel organized and modeled in fashion shows featuring Manila's elite designers Renee Salud and Patis Tesoro. Eventually, her exploits in fashion brought her to the nationwide beauty pageant Binibining Pilipinas 1998 (Miss Philippines).

Education and Career Charmel graduated with honors, with a bachelor's degree in International Studies in Miriam College (formerly Maryknoll College), took up systems development courses, and started her career as a business analyst. She immigrated to Australia where she worked in various roles in information technology, with a career spanning 15 years.

Entrepreneurship, Investing and Trading Charmel was brought up with an entrepreneurial mindset. As a youngster, she sold "halo-halo" (a popular cold dessert) in the neighborhood, designed and marketed specialty T-shirts, and organized events. She first invested in real estate on various residential and commercial projects in Australia and New Zealand. She then traded shares and options. She uses band trading, trend following, spreading, and inter-market analysis (applying relationship of forex to other assets). She has taken advanced workshops in peak performance, business planning, and systems development. Her current trading focus is for protecting shareholdings and generating income using options strategies and developing a system for forex trading.

Want to know more?

Join the growing community of women traders by visiting my website at www.highheeledtraders.com, where you can read my blog posts and watch videos.

Updated regularly :

- Market Fashions – what are the raging issues in the financial market.

- Events – tea parties, special events.0

- Readers' Share – what other women are thinking about regarding their trades.

Twitter : @hiheeldtraders

Email: charmel@highheeledtraders.com

_____

Index

Made in the USA
Middletown, DE
03 July 2022

68199595R00186